I0789096

How to Trick People into Doing the Right Thing

Also by Byron Kennard

Nothing Can Be Done
Everything is Possible

You Can't Fool Mother Nature:
The Once and Future Triumph of Environmentalism

How to Trick People into Doing the Right Thing

BYRON KENNARD

How to Trick People into Doing the Right Thing

Copyright (c) 2020 Byron Kennard

All rights reserved.

ISBN: 9798666616413

Published by
The Two Josephines Press
2220 20th Street, NW
Washington, DC 20009

bckennard@aol.com

ByronKennard.com

Byron's books available
at *Amazon.com*

Book and cover design: Joe Handy

Dear Reader,

Is it your perception that the whole world is going to hell in a hand-basket? *Good!* I applaud your perspicacity. You and I are starting off on the same page *figuratively and literally* — which is devoutly to be desired.

It means I don't have to fart around, lamenting and lambasting the foolishness and destructiveness of climate deniers, covid-19 deniers, and the anti-science nincompoops.

It means I don't have to waste your time and mine weeping and wailing over the damage being done to democracy and the rule of law by tin-horn demagogues, greedy and corrupt oligarchs, and faux populist zealots.

It also means I can cut to the chase and divulge the matter in question which impelled the writing of this book:

> *Is there a way that social progress*
> *and social justice can proceed*
> *when the whole world is rapidly*
> *going to hell in a hand-basket?*

The surprising answer? *Yes, there is a way!*
But it's a damned tricky business, as you are about to learn. The trick is not to bang on democracy's front door, demanding to be let in. At present, that entry is effectively barred. And so long as our democracy is severed by political polarization and crippled by corruption, that entry will remain barred.

The trick is to *sneak in* through the back door.

— The Author

TABLE OF CONTENTS

PRELUDE

"Honest Abe" Pulls a Fast One;
How Emancipation got Proclaimed   1

PART ONE

The Lessons I Learned
In Sunday School   5

   Always tell the truth

   Practice clemency: "Forgive thy enemies"

   Seek justice, especially for those less fortunate

   Place faith in reason

   Collaborate with others to pursue the common good

   Practice moderation in all things

   Cling to ideals, no matter what: "To thy own self, be true"

PART TWO

*The Perils of the Lessons I Learned
In Sunday School*

Machiavelli:
On the Perils of Truth-telling   9

Julius Caesar:
On the Perils of Clemency   12

King Richard III:
On the Perils of Just Rule   14

Cicero:
On the Perils of Faith in Reason   17

America's Founding Fathers:
On the Perils of Collaboration   18

Madame Roland:
On the Perils of Moderation   21

Rosa Luxembourg:
On the Perils of Idealism   22

PART THREE

Tricked by Political Magicians   25

Tricked by democratic pretenses:
Pericles, *a great aristocrat, acquired
vast power by pretending to be a
democrat.*   29

Tricked by a woman's determination
to be taken seriously: **Aspasia,** *the
mistress of Pericles was the teacher of
Socrates.*   31

Tricked by republican pretenses:
The **Emperor Augustus,** *a military
dictator, exercised power by pretending
to be a devout republican.*   33

Tricked by ladylike demeanor (#1):
Livia, *the demure, dutiful wife of
Emperor Augustus called the shots
from behind the scenes.*   36

Tricked by cross-dressing:
In fifteenth century France,
Joan of Arc *wore the pants.*   37

Tricked by a woman who refused to
make up her mind: **Queen Elizabeth I**
*achieved the greatest reign in English
history by ruling through indirection.*   40

Tricked by being given "enough rope":
*How **Akbar the Great** found a way to
establish religious toleration
throughout his vast Mughal empire.*   44

Tricked by a hat: **Benjamin Franklin**
*and his coonskin cap made the success
of the American revolution possible.*   46

Tricked by a tiger changing its stripes (# 1):
*When **President Thomas Jefferson**
conveniently put aside his bedrock
principles to expand the nation.*   49

Tricked by a change in the cast of
characters: *How **Talleyrand** saved
France from the destructive fury of
Napoleon's enemies.*   50

Tricked by faith in the U.S. Constitution:
Frederick Douglass *genuinely loved
America's founding documents --
"all men are created equal"!*   54

Tricked by faith in religion:
*In Christianity, **Harriet Tubman**
found the courage to perform miracles.*   60

Tricked by compassionate conservatism:
*British Prime Minister **Disraeli** persuaded
Tories to enact and administer Whig
policies and programs.*   63

Tricked by theatrics: *Was **Franklin D.
Roosevelt** America's greatest actor?*   69

Tricked by unladylike behavior:
***Mother Jones** put women and children
in the front lines of protest marches by
striking coalminers.*   71

Tricked by sexual innuendo and double
entendres: ***Mae West** launched a
worldwide sexual revolution.*   75

Tricked by the use of a demigod as
bargaining chip: *How **General Douglas
MacArthur** managed to establish
democracy in postwar Japan.*   82

Trickery by simplicity:
***Gandhi** as a political showman.*   89

Trickery by grandeur: **Charles de Gaulle** *as a political showman.* 93

Tricked by mumbling: **Dwight Eisenhower** *deliberately concealed his strengths so his foes would underestimate him.* 99

Tricked by a tiger changing its stripes (# 2): **Lyndon Johnson,** *a southern racist, became the greatest civil rights President since Abraham Lincoln.* 102

Tricked by a tiger changing its stripes (# 3): **Nixon** *went to China.* 106

Tricked by ladylike demeanor (#2): *How* **Mrs. Ronald Reagan** *ended the Cold War without firing a shot.* 110

Tricked by pop culture: **Ellen DeGeneres** *and gay rights advocates built public support for same-sex marriage by scorning conventional politics.* 113

Tricked by youth: Fifteen-year-old **Greta Thunberg** *asks world leaders a simple question and, in doing so, exposes the fallacy of economics.* 118

POSTLUDE *125*

APOLOGIES *131*

ABOUT THE AUTHOR *133*

ACKNOWLEDGMENTS *137*

NOTES ON THE IMAGES *139*

DEDICATION

*This book is dedicated to everyone who hates
and despises (in their terms, not mine):
bitches, chinks, coons, dykes, fags, fairies,
feminazis, gooks, hippies, injuns, jigaboos,
kikes, (the N-word), pansies, queers, redskins,
sluts, spics, trannys, tree huggers, uppity
Blacks, and wetbacks.*

*I make this dedication in the earnest hope that
at least some of these assholes will
soon be tricked into doing the right thing.*

How to Trick People into Doing the Right Thing

"Perhaps some of you will think that I am jesting."

— **Socrates**, *at his trial*

How to Trick People into Doing the Right Thing

PRELUDE

"Honest Abe" pulls a fast one:
How Emancipation got Proclaimed

Lincoln's most notable Presidential act was, of course, issuing the Emancipation Proclamation that freed the slaves. It was also the most devious act of his Presidency.

Lincoln could not have freed the slaves in his capacity as President of the United States. He lacked the authority. And, besides, Lincoln — who despised slavery — had nevertheless declared time and again he was fighting the war to preserve the union, not to abolish slavery. These declarations were politically essential to Lincoln's leadership because most people in the North were willing to support a war to preserve the union — but not a war to abolish slavery.

However, as Commander in Chief of an army then engaged on the field of combat, Lincoln could invoke "war powers" that gave him the right to seize and destroy enemy property for reasons of military necessity. (Remember, at this time, legally, slaves were considered property.)

Since the Southerners used slaves to support their armies in the field, Lincoln justified the Emancipation Proclamation as a "fit and necessary war measure" to cripple the Confederacy's war effort.

What an astute maneuver! In one fell swoop, Lincoln silenced the voices of the many Northerners (perhaps most) who didn't support emancipation, but who — given Lincoln's coup — felt compelled to support it as a war measure.

In *Lincoln's Political Thought*, the author, Professor George Kateb, makes this astounding observation: "Lincoln's political life illustrates the unsettling truth that in democratic politics — perhaps in all politics — it is nearly impossible to do the right thing for the right reasons, honestly stated."

This book offers a mountain of evidence — all drawn from world history — to substantiate Professor Kateb's unsettling truth.

How to Trick People into Doing the Right Thing

PART ONE

The Lessons I Learned in Sunday School

I was a prissy little boy, just the sort who became the pet of my Sunday school teacher. Bless her heart, she wanted to make me a good man and a good citizen too. She aimed to instill in me a desire to always do the right thing. To this end, she taught me that I should:

- Always tell the truth, bearing in mind that honesty is the best policy;

- Forgive my enemies: "To err is human, to forgive divine," she told me, quoting Alexander Pope;

- Strive to see that justice is done to others, especially to those in need and less fortunate than myself;

- Place my faith in reason and my trust in the rule of law — that's the surest path to good citizenship;

- Learn to work well with other people; to cooperate with them in the pursuit of the common good, which is the ultimate aim of civic virtue;

- Practice moderation in all things;

- Cling resolutely to my ideals no matter how hard it gets. "To thy own self be true," she instructed me.

I took all these lessons to heart and vowed to live my life in full accord with them. I would make my Sunday school teacher proud of me, by golly.

Me as a Community Organizer

When I grew up, I decided to become a community organizer, a job I conceived of as instilling in others a desire to always do the right thing. My Sunday school teacher would have been thrilled to hear this.

Alas, as a community organizer, I was to learn people are not much inclined to do the right thing. They've got other fish to fry — literally. For starters, procuring three square meals a day. Other preoccupations include getting laid, getting rich, and getting even with their enemies. Who's got the time and energy left over to do the right thing?

Oh dear, life is not lived in a Sunday school, I discovered. On top of that, my passion for virtue was being undermined by a second passion, which led me down another path, much rockier.

Me as a Lifelong History Buff

Growing up, I always had my nose stuck in a history book. Reading history was my passion (and still is). But what I learned from history books was different from what I had been taught in the rarefied atmosphere of the Sunday schoolroom.

Oh, what a stern teacher history is! By comparison, my Sunday school teacher was a sweetheart, a perfect angel. She spared the rod; history keeps rapping me hard across the knuckles. And not only that; history keeps rubbing my nose in a heap of reeking reality.

Reading history forced me to realize the virtues taught me in Sunday school can be downright dangerous. Practitioners of virtue — especially ardent ones — can be impoverished, arrested, thrown in prison, and tortured. And with surprising frequency, virtuous people can even be murdered.

"If you want to tell people the truth, make them laugh," said Oscar Wilde. "Otherwise, they'll kill you." (Caution: Wilde did make people laugh, but they killed him anyway.)

PART TWO

The Perils of the Lessons I Learned In Sunday School

To illustrate this dismal state of affairs, I ransacked the history books, and for each lesson in uprightness taught me in Sunday school — honesty, justice, clemency, faith in reason, moderation, working in harmony with others, and resolute idealism — I selected a famous leader whom I thought best exemplified that particular quality. And — Lord, have mercy! — Look at what happened to them!

Machiavelli: *On the Perils of Truth-telling*

To me, Niccolò Machiavelli (1469 – 1527) is one of the greatest truth-tellers who ever lived — when it comes to politics, perhaps the greatest. He was scrupulously honest and unafraid to go where his honesty took him.

His famous (infamous) book, *The Prince,* is a short treatise on how to acquire power, create a state, and keep it. It is a guide for political action based on the lessons of history and his own experience as a foreign secretary in Florence, the republican city-state that was his beloved homeland.

A passionate patriot, his aim was to preserve Florence's freedom at a time when it was threatened from every side.

To this end, Machiavelli recorded a thoroughly honest description of how states and societies *really* operate — not how we're *told* they operate or how they're *supposed* to operate.

He believed we'd be better off if we perceived how people *really are* as distinct from the moralizing claptrap about how they *ought to be.* But the truths Machiavelli told were hard for most people to swallow. To make the point, here are three examples of Machiavelli's unpalatable truths:

"The fact is that a man who wants to act virtuously in every way necessarily comes to grief among so many who are not virtuous."

"Men are so stupid and concerned with their present needs, they will always let themselves be deceived."

"Of mankind we may say in general they are fickle, hypocritical, and greedy of gain."

Obviously, this kind of talk is no way to win friends and influence people, most of whom *prefer* moralizing claptrap to the truth. (Still the case today, five hundred years later.)

Machiavelli was deprived of office in 1512 by the Medici. He was imprisoned where he was tortured by the *strappado,* a form of torture wherein the victim's hands are tied behind his back. The victim is then suspended by a rope attached to the wrists, typically resulting in dislocated shoulders.

Luckily, he survived this torture and eventually won his freedom. But he was exiled from his beloved Florence, forced to live on his father's dilapidated farm where he died, miserable and impoverished.

Poor Machiavelli! He was the most amiable of men and a devout humanist. But for centuries following his death, the name

Machiavelli was a synonym for the devil. Down through history, his name has been synonymous with amorality, cunning, deceit, duplicity, and unscrupulous bad faith in politics and statecraft. To be called *Machiavellian* is a grave insult.

Julius Caesar: *On the Perils of Clemency*

Soon after seizing Rome and assuming dictatorial powers in 49 BC, Caesar attempted a bold experiment in the exercise of clemency. Rather than slaying his defeated foes, Caesar pardoned most of them; and, what's more, he allowed them to keep their property. These enlightened actions won praise from Cicero, who was Caesar's bitter critic but who, nonetheless, described him as "mild and merciful by nature."

Caesar even promoted some of his enemies to high public office. For example, Marcus Brutus and Gaius Cassius were not only pardoned but elevated to praetorships, the second highest ranking posts in the Republic.

This clemency was unprecedented in Rome. His predecessor, Lucius Cornelius Sulla (who ruled 82 – 80 BC) set the precedent for Caesar's dictatorship, but showing his enemies mercy wasn't Sulla's style. Quite the contrary.

When Sulla took control of Rome, he set out mercilessly to slay all those whom he regarded as his enemies. As Plutarch noted, "Sulla now began to make blood flow, and he filled the city with deaths without number or limit . . . Husbands were butchered in the arms of their wives, sons in the arms of their mothers."

Caesar's clemency is in startling contrast to these vile images, but what good did it do him? Historians estimate that as many as sixty individuals were involved in the conspiracy to assassinate Caesar. At least a majority of these conspirators were former foes whom he had pardoned.

Even some of Caesar's friends and trusted colleagues were in on the plot. They had grown convinced his dictatorship would be the end of the Republic, which, though decrepit and corrupt, was still cherished by some Roman patriots. Their way of saying "thank you" was to take him by surprise and stab him with a dagger. He was stabbed twenty-three times.

"Caesar's example suggests that leaders either need to be loved or feared," warns historian and classicist Barry Strauss in his book *The Death of Caesar: The Story of History's Most Famous Assassination.* While I can't recommend that our modern politicos and CEOs expropriate and murder their opponents after acceding to power, thinking twice about extending the olive branch makes just as much sense now as it did in the last years of the Roman republic."

Richard III: *On the Perils of Just Rule*

Traditionally, the Coronation Oath administered to a new English King includes this exchange:

How many Kings in English history actually made good on this oath? How many actually caused law and justice to be executed in all their judgments?

In my search of history, I found only one: Richard III, the most maligned monarch in English history, the victim of Tudor propaganda after his defeat by Henry Tudor and his gruesome death at the Battle of Bosworth in 1485.

Richard was the first king to take the Coronation Oath in English; and he ordered that his laws be published in English, so they could be read by people other than the educated classes who could read Latin.

In his brief two-year reign, Richard III enacted important reforms, including the Land Tenure Act that helped safeguard the property rights of commoners, which were often infringed by powerful nobles. He also established administrative methods for hearing the petitions of poor people, who normally could not afford to seek assistance from the law.

To extend justice to the underprivileged usually involves reducing the might of the overprivileged, whose power and wealth are mostly derived from exploitation of the underprivileged.

So, ruling justly conflicts with the greedy interests of the landed aristocracy, and that comes at a price. Richard was betrayed at Bosworth by aristocrat-led English armies that were there, supposedly, to support him.

After death, Richard's body was stripped of armor and slung over a horse to be taken to Leicester for public display. There his body was mocked, mutilated, and subjected to acts of ritual humiliation, including being sodomized by a sword.

Cicero: *On the Perils of Faith in Reason*

In his first campaign for public office, Cicero, Rome's greatest politician, learned "the people would rather be lied to than told no." And that was just for starters.

His experience of politics would lead him to observe: "Men decide far more problems by hate, love, lust, rage, sorrow, joy, hope, fear, illusion, or some other inward emotion," he declared, "than by reality, authority, any legal standard, judicial precedent, or statute." So much for reason!

Cicero's efforts to oppose tyranny and to preserve the Roman republic ultimately failed. The victorious tyrants outlawed him. He was captured, killed, and his body mutilated. His head and hands were cut off and nailed on the rostra, the speakers' platform at the Roman Forum.

America's Founding Fathers: *On the Perils of Collaboration*

What a splendid example of collaboration is provided by America's Founding Fathers! A distinct political elite, they worked together with remarkable wisdom and foresight, and their joint achievement is universally regarded as a high point in all history.

Having collaborated to produce this grand and glorious achievement, one might think the Founding Fathers would spend the rest of their lives resting on their laurels and honoring one another. But no! They spent the rest of their lives engaged in bitter rivalries, despising and betraying one another, almost without exception. Indeed, it's hard to keep track of *who hated who.*

Although Thomas Jefferson, John Adams, and Benjamin Franklin famously collaborated to write the *Declaration of Independence,* as time went on, Jefferson came to hate Adams, and vice versa. As for Franklin, he called Adams a hothead who was "sometimes absolutely mad." For his part, Adams called Franklin the "Old Conjuror;" and, according to Jefferson, Adams' feelings for Franklin were "poisonous."

Alexander Hamilton and James Madison were bosom buddies, of course, when they cowrote the hugely influential *Federalist Papers* and, in 1787, when they orchestrated the call for a constitutional convention in Philadelphia. But in 1792, Madison abandoned his bosom buddy and partnered with Jefferson to blacken

Hamilton's reputation, calling him a monarchist. For his part, Hamilton denounced this partnership as "dangerous to the union, peace and happiness of the Country."

Most tragically, Hamilton, a founding father, was to be murdered by another, Aaron Burr.

Even Washington, the peerless hero, was subjected to such abuse. After he left office, Washington was convinced his Administration had been undermined and even betrayed by Jefferson, Madison, and Monroe — once his trusted collaborators — and he refused to speak to any of them ever again.

Later, when Jefferson became President, he insisted on paying a courtesy call on the Widow Washington at Mount Vernon, a visit she didn't want because she despised Jefferson. But she felt unable to refuse the request since Jefferson was the President.

When the visit was over and Jefferson had departed, Martha Washington confided to a friend that the experience had been the worst thing she'd had to endure since the death of her husband.

Madame Roland: *On the Perils of Moderation*

In the midst of a violent revolution, an open mind can lead to a severed head.

Consider the fate of Marie-Jeanne Phlippon Roland, a leader of the Girondist faction in the French Revolution. The Girondins were political moderates who stood for a Republican form of government. They were committed to political and economic liberties, so therefore unwilling to support the extreme revolutionary measures advocated by the radical Jacobins.

Girondins opposed the execution of King Louis XVI, a fight they lost to the Jacobins. They also opposed the Reign of Terror and tried to stop it but tragically failed, thus sealing their own doom. They paid with their heads.

Madame Roland is famous for declaring as she placed her head on the guillotine's block: "Oh liberty, what crimes are committed in thy name!" (She is also famous for declaring, "The more I see of men, the more I admire dogs.")

Rosa Luxembourg: *On the Perils of Idealism*

There probably has never been a group of individuals so earnestly and passionately devoted to the ideal of universal justice as the early socialists in the late 19th and early 20th centuries. They were mainly Jewish intellectuals — many of them brilliant as well as selfless and tireless. With all their hearts, they believed a better world was possible — and even within our grasp. So, it was worth fighting for no matter what. Many of these high-minded idealists who clung so fiercely to their ideals paid with their lives.

Most notable amongst them was Rosa Luxembourg (1871 – 1919), a German-Polish Marxist and revolutionary who was a great orator and a prolific writer. Luxembourg was a humanitarian Marxist, democratic-minded and with a strong libertarian bent. She stoutly opposed Bolshevik authoritarianism and party control by a small elite.

The early socialists earnestly believed the coming of socialism would put an end to warfare. They believed in *the revolutionary mass strike idea*. Socialism, they claimed, would enable industrial workers everywhere to reach international solidarity. This solidarity would prevent nation states from going to war because workers would strike, closing industry down, thus depriving nation states of the means to conduct war.

Luxembourg was the outstanding protagonist of this idea, and so she was crushed in 1914 when German socialists abandoned it to support Germany's entry into World War I. At the same time, socialist parties in France and most other countries strongly supported their national war effort. The socialist ideal was trumped by a surge in national patriotism and love of the Fatherland, which many workers shared along with the industrialists who were exploiting them.

So much for solidarity.

Luxembourg, aghast, saw workers and their leaders line up behind their respective governments ready to take part in the slaughter. This was, she felt, the complete destruction of her life's work. Actually, when she heard the news, she had a grave psychological breakdown. Eventually, however, she recovered and began to agitate furiously for a return to the revolutionary mass strike idea — and with some success when Germany lost the war and social order was disintegrating.

This was her doom.

Rosa Luxembourg was arrested in Berlin on January 15, 1919, by members of the Free Corps (Freikorps), a loose assemblage of right-wing paramilitary groups. She was clubbed, beaten senseless, and shot. Her body was thrown in the Landwehr Canal in Berlin. It was found and identified six months later.

PART THREE

Tricked by Political Magicians

As I stated in the Author's note at the beginning, if social progress is to be achieved in this cold, cruel world then we must rely — with some frequency — on acts of deviousness by political leaders to get the job done. That's the knotty premise of this book. Why is this so?

Part of me wishes to respond by simply and emphatically declaring *people are no damn good*. I'd get a kick out of saying so, but that blanket condemnation isn't really the case.

The problem is that *enough people are no damn good enough of the time* to endanger all that we hold dear, including life, liberty, and the pursuit of happiness. They're the rotten apples in the barrel of life.

If there were no ways to counter the spoliation caused by rotten apples, civilization would have collapsed long ago. But — thank your lucky stars — civilization has *not* collapsed. Moreover, I contend that — in some key ways — civilization is actually progressing.

I write in defense of deviousness. Great leaders frequently use it to trick people into doing the right thing — and for that we can all be grateful.

Now, everybody knows bad guys frequently pull tricks — *dirty* tricks — to do bad things. But few people know good guys pull tricks too — *benevolent* tricks — to do good things.

Really great leaders have found ways to run rings around the bad guys. They've learned how to confuse and confound them, to distract and divert them, and to manipulate and mislead them. Naturally, these prodigious manipulations cannot be performed by rank amateurs. Much talent and skill is required.

Now — of course — we need leaders who are able, wise, altruistic, far-sighted, and devoted to social progress. Nobody quarrels with that. But, virtue alone does not suffice — not when you're locked in battle with the bad guys. So, in addition to virtue, I argue that we need leaders who are cunning, audacious, intrepid, and a bit shameless and cynical (but not too much so). It also helps if these leaders are really good actors.

"All successful leaders are to varying degrees magicians and actors," writes Jonathan Fenby in his book, *The General: Charles de Gaulle and the France He Saved.* To back up this assertion, Fenby has an ideal example in his subject: Charles de Gaulle. As a political magician, de Gaulle was a lollapalooza, no less. That's because he devoutly believed his own publicity.

Fenby writes of the General, "Though it opened him to mockery from those who saw him as ridiculously self-important, the key to his greatness lay in a single factor: *his genuine belief that he incarnated France.*"

Of course, de Gaulle possessed a peerless reputation and enormous prestige as a French war hero in World War II, but his sense of self-importance soared beyond that into the stratosphere. It seems de Gaulle *actually believed* he was some combination of Joan of Arc, Louis XIV, and Napoleon Bonaparte.

You might think this was a dangerous delusion that would land him in the funny farm, but it didn't. Instead, in 1959, it landed him in the Élysée Palace, the official residence of the President of the French Republic. Eighty percent of the French electorate supported his election to the post.

De Gaulle's unashamed conviction he embodied the grandeur of French civilization actually helped him convince the French people his act was the real thing. The French lapped it up as if it were Dom Pérignon.

Now, not all the historical figures I've profiled in this book were so self-entranced they fooled themselves while they were fooling everybody else. As you will see in the profiles that follow, most were keenly aware they were engaged in devious behavior, and they delighted in the play-acting that was involved.

This story is as old as time. So — what better place to start than at the beginning of recorded history?

Tricked by democratic pretenses:
Pericles, a great aristocrat, acquired vast power by pretending to be a democrat.

Pericles (495 – 429 BC), the Athenian statesman, has long been hailed as the first great democratic leader in Western civilization, but he is also the first great political boss. He makes Boss Tweed of Tammany Hall look like a piker.

Here's the story: For all its glory, Athen's experiment in democracy was a messy and unstable affair, riven by continuous strife between the city's wealthy aristocrats and its great mass of poor citizens. (Sound familiar?) Into this muddle steps Pericles, a wealthy aristocrat gifted with extraordinary political genius. Pericles uses his gift to govern Athens through backstairs management so deftly that he alone called almost all the shots.

Here's how he did it. Thanks to reforms introduced by Pericles, *thetes* — the lowest social class of citizens in Athens — were granted the right to hold public office. Thus, thousands of landless, poor Athenian males were enabled to participate in the democracy.

Pericles changed the rules so citizens were paid for jury duty and other civic services. This enabled the poor to serve in such posts. In the past, only the rich had undertaken such duties because they could afford to serve without pay. He even subsidized the costs of theater admission so the poor could attend.

Is it any surprise the poor voted in massive numbers to support Pericles' political agenda? As the historian Thucydides described Athens during Pericles' time, "In name democracy, but in fact the rule of one man."

Pericles' one-man rule operated behind a shield of democratic pretenses; and he, personally, pretended to be a democrat, a ruse he pulled off superbly. (Like most other great political tricksters, Pericles was a first-class actor.)

Pericles was so devoted to serving the city's interests he appeared to neglect his own interests, though they were substantial. The *thetes* were suitably impressed. He lived modestly, even humbly, never putting on airs. In his entire career, it was said that he attended only one social event, which he left early.

He ruled Athens for thirty years and to civilization's immense benefit. During "the Age of Pericles," he forged "the glory that was Greece" — achieving colossal advances in science, philosophy, democracy, art and architecture, poetry and drama.

Tricked by a woman's determination to be taken seriously: *Aspasia, the mistress of Pericles was the teacher of Socrates.*

The glory that was Greece did not shine brightly on women. In Athens, the hub of the classical age, they were kept in the dark. Women were not allowed to acquire an education, to vote, or to participate in public affairs in any way. A woman was expected to stay home, keep house, and bear children.

Then how on earth does one explain the life and career Aspasia of Miletus (470 BC – 400 BC)? She was a scholar and philosopher who became one of the most vivid figures in classical Athens. She played a key role in the intellectual development of Greece during its golden age.

Given the times she lived in, it's hard to believe Aspasia existed. What magic did she possess?

Well, to start with she was unusually beautiful; and she won the heart — and the ear — of Pericles, the most powerful statesman of classical Athens. Their relationship was scandalous because they remained unmarried and because of *her determination to be treated as an equal —* which Pericles gladly did.

As his consort, Aspasia lived at the very center of Athenian political life. Her home was something of a hub for prominent Athenian figures. Plato admired her intelligence and wit.

She tutored Socrates when he was a boy,
teaching him rhetoric. Later, Socrates was to
credit her with the writing of some of Pericles'
best and most famous speeches.

If Pericles is the first great man in Western
history, then Aspasia is the first great woman.
She deserves a full share of the abundant glory
that a grateful humankind has bestowed on
Pericles.

Tricked by republican pretenses:
***The Emperor Augustus, a military dictator,
exercised power by pretending to be a devout
republican.***

Augustus Caesar (63 BC – AD 14) was first
and greatest Emperor of Rome. Coming to
power after a century of civil war, he declared
his aim to be the restoration of the Republic.

This was a bunch of hooey, of course.
Augustus ruled as a military dictator. (Where
Pericles succeeded by pretending to be a
democrat, Augustus succeeded by pretending
to be a republican.)

A staunch conservative, Augustus knew that it is better (and far easier) to revive a state of affairs that previously existed than to construct and impose some new state of affairs. Besides, for many Romans, the image of the beloved old republic still glowed brightly in their memories. To this end, Augustus retained all the outward forms of the Republic — the Senate and so on — and he made a big show of personally conforming with old traditions and practices.

Augustus declined to accept titles, honors, and offices voted him by the restored Senate while appearing regularly before the body offering to resign the various posts he did hold and begging to be allowed to return to private life. Naturally, the Senate wouldn't hear of it. (No wonder. It was filled with men appointed by Augustus.)

Augustus displayed a pious respect for religious tradition. He called for a return to traditional family values and saw to it laws were passed to regulate sexual behavior and to punish adultery.

But, of course, Augustus only *pretended* to restore the Republic. In truth, he governed as a de facto dictator — a reality no one could ignore. Nevertheless, the Roman public went along with the trick because they passionately desired the order and stability Augustus's 41-year-long reign delivered.

Augustus's extraordinary trickery inaugurated the *Pax Romana*, the longest period of uninterrupted peace in recorded history.

Tricked by ladylike demeanor (#1):
Livia, the demure, dutiful wife of Emperor Augustus, called the shots from behind the scenes.

Augustus lived with his wife Livia Drusilla (58 BC — AD 29) in a modest house where she played the role of a loving, dutiful, and even old-fashioned wife, taking care of the household, spinning, weaving, and making her husband's clothes herself.

Livia was one of the women in history who exercised power while living in the shadow of a strong leader, serving silently as his advisor and confidante, respected for her cunning. (Think of her as the Nancy Reagan of her day.) While she served the empire as a symbol of the loyal Roman wife, behind the scenes at the imperial court, the old girl was pulling the strings.

Tricked by cross-dressing: *In fifteenth century France, Joan of Arc wore the pants.*

In the Middle Ages, the sons of the nobility were raised to be warriors, almost from the time they could walk. One of the most important and difficult things they had to learn was how to ride and command a warhorse. This was *de rigueur*.

In those days, the most powerful weapon in existence was an armored knight on horseback wielding a lance. It was said that, in battle, one such knight was the equivalent of eighty men on foot.

It took *years* for boys to learn how to do this. Joan of Arc (1412 — 1431), a 17-year-old illiterate peasant girl, learned how to do it in six weeks. *What a pucelle!*

Joan of Arc changed history by bending gender. Practically overnight, this peasant girl became a warrior, doing things only men could do. She donned male body armor, wielded a lance, mounted a warhorse, and led armies into battle, winning nine major military victories.

Nobody then or now can explain how she managed to do these things. She is one of the great enigmas of all time. And her enigmatic image exerts great power to this day, appealing strongly to many kinds of people.

Joan is venerated as a heroine by French nationalists. She is a saint canonized by the Catholic Church (so far, we know, the only cross-dresser to be so honored).

For centuries, women have looked on Joan as an inspiring example of a powerful, independent woman. Her symbolic power as a woman who took history into her hands resonated especially among women *fighting for the right to vote*. During the struggle to achieve voting rights for women, Joan became the symbol of the movement. Suffragette parades were led by women costumed as Joan of Arc and mounted on a white horse.

Contemporary feminists invoke her as an emblem of the non-traditional "new woman" in the modern world. LGBT activists proudly claim her as one of their own — and they might be right to do so.

In 1430, Joan was captured by the English and put on trial. The court records show Joan's judges found her transvestism repugnant and demanded she wear women's clothing. Joan refused, knowing full well her defiance would condemn her to death. Thus it was the 19-year-old French peasant-girl-turned-soldier was burned at the stake for the crime of dressing as a man.

Tricked by a woman who refused to make up her mind: *Queen Elizabeth I achieved greatest reign in English history by ruling through indirection.*

When Elizabeth I came to the throne in 1558 at age 25, she was surrounded on all sides by men who were determined to dominate her. Mind you, these were not the Queen's *foes* but her *supporters* — her wise councilors, her loyal courtiers, and even her pining would-be lovers.

In a man's world, even an anointed Queen is, nonetheless, a mere woman dependent on male wisdom and strength. So male domination of Her Majesty would be, of course, for her own good — not to mention the good of her realm.

These males were in for a surprise. They'd never encountered a female like Elizabeth Tudor. Here was a female determined not to be dominated by men; instead, *she was determined to dominate them.*

From the start, the Queen's overriding aim was to rule in her own right — that is, *as a woman.* Such a thing was unheard of. It practically constituted a sacrilege. Thus, in pursuit of her aim, Elizabeth stood alone, opposed by the whole world. But even when the whole world opposed her, she zigged and zagged until she found a way to get her way.

This brings us to the mainspring of Elizabeth's career, the thing on which everything turns: her refusal to marry. Think of it: the whole world expected her to marry — nay! — the whole world *demanded* she marry.

Elizabeth's subjects, high-born and low, beseeched her to wed and start churning out babies (boys preferably, of course). God in heaven, what if she were to die childless and without a legitimate heir?! This prospect had the English scared out of their wits — and for good reason. Instantly, a hodgepodge of claimants to the throne would emerge to violently contest the succession.

A civil war over religion between Catholics and Protestants was almost certain to break out, probably leading to the invasion of England by France or Spain. In this turmoil, English Protestants had every reason to fear that their property, their liberties, and their lives were at stake.

What an imbroglio! But our shyster of a Queen managed to finesse the situation in no time flat. The old girl had a couple of tricks up her sleeve.

Sure, everybody in the world agreed Elizabeth *should* marry; but when it came to the crucial question of exactly *whom* she should marry, this agreement burst into smithereens. Should she marry a Catholic or a Protestant? A Frenchman or a Spaniard? A foreigner or a subject?

This indecision *on the world's part* was a boon to Elizabeth. It put her in the driver's seat. The whole world couldn't force her to marry if it couldn't agree on *who* she was to marry. After all, the poor woman couldn't marry a regiment of men. She could marry only *one*. Who was this lucky chap to be? No consensus on this question could be formed. It wasn't in the cards, not even remotely.

Hallelujah, Elizabeth was, in effect, *liberated!* In this situation, she could do what *she* wanted, not what others wanted her to do. What she *didn't want* was being forced to submit to the authority of a husband, as tradition then dictated. Elizabeth was adamant about having no part of this. "I will have but one mistress here, and no master," she declared. That's what she wanted, and that's what she got.

Elizabeth became one of the most celebrated and brilliant figures in world history. Many Britons consider her the greatest monarch England ever had. Many historians consider her reign — dubbed by history as the Elizabethan *era* — to be England's golden age. Her patronage of the arts led to the flowering of the English Renaissance — Shakespeare and all that.

Tricked by being given "enough rope:" *How Akbar the Great found a way to establish religious toleration throughout his vast Mughal empire.*

Akbar the Great (1542 – 1605) made his name as the Muslim conqueror of Hindu India. But Hindus were unwilling to accept foreign Muslim rule and were prepared to fight for their autonomy. Akbar thus prepared to embark on a monumental task of gaining the consent of the Hindu majority.

This compelled Akbar to wage war against the mullahs (experts in Muslim religious matters) for control over social and political policy in his empire. The mullahs were determined to impose orthodox Islam on all of the Hindus. This was a recipe for continuous social disorder, unacceptable to Akbar.

When powerful Muslim clerics confronted Akbar insisting they, and not he, had the power to control religious practice in the Empire, Akbar responded by pretending to agree with them. All he asked, he told them, was that they go off by themselves and forge a plan they could all agree on. Then they should return, he said, bringing their plan to him, which he would then institute. But they never returned with a plan. Why? Because they could never come to agreement amongst themselves. So, Akbar dismissed them and then continued and expanded his policy of religious tolerance.

Akbar laid the foundation for 150 years of a multi-religious empire under Mughal rule.

Tricked by a hat: *How Benjamin Franklin and his coonskin cap made the success of the American revolution possible.*

Benjamin Franklin (1706 – 1790). In 1778, Franklin was in France attempting to secure support for the American revolution. Going about in society he didn't wear a wig or powder his hair like everyone else. Instead he wore a coonskin cap to keep his bald head warm. This won over influential French intellectuals and aristocratic reformers who were enthralled by images of republican simplicity. Franklin was a huge hit with the French, who saw him as the natural man and embodiment of reason.

While Franklin appeared to be all benevolence and bonhomie, he was actually a creature of vast cunning and guile. That's how he managed to talk the French out of $14 billion — in today's money — to finance the American revolution, money without which the revolution probably would have failed. (This was money the French could ill afford to give. They were tottering on bankruptcy.)

Franklin secured this aid while circumventing vicious infighting amongst his American colleagues and treacherous backroom dealings at Versailles. He operated on the sly, often misleading his quarreling colleagues. These included the estimable John Adams — an "authentic" man if there ever was one — honest to a fault — and therefore worse than useless in diplomacy. For his part, the principled Adams was contemptuous of Franklin, whom he described as "the greatest imposter on earth." Adams ranted about Franklin's secrecy, cunning, and deviousness to anyone who would listen.

Adams is not alone in his harsh judgment of Franklin. Murray Rothbard, a famed economist and political theorist, deprecates Franklin's achievements and accentuates his peccadilloes. He finds in the sly Dr. Franklin "a sinister, subversive devil . . . an opportunist par excellence . . . cunning . . . fawning . . . meddling . . . opportunistic hedonist . . ."

But even Rothbard can't help offering Franklin a left-handed compliment, commenting that, "The wily old tactician Franklin proved to be a master at the intricacies of lying, bamboozling, and intrigue that form the warp and woof of diplomacy."

As I read history, Franklin's deviousness was what it took to obtain the French support that enabled America to win the revolutionary war. Thanks to the wily old tactician, there were more French soldiers on the battlefield at Yorktown than American.

Tricked by a tiger changing its stripes (#1): *When President Thomas Jefferson conveniently put aside his bedrock principles to expand the nation.*

President Thomas Jefferson (1743 – 1826) was a strict Constitutionalist and the original champion of small government. But this tiger changed his stripes in 1803 when the chance to make the Louisiana Purchase came along. What a deal! It doubled the size of the country and — at 13 cents an acre — was an incredible bargain.

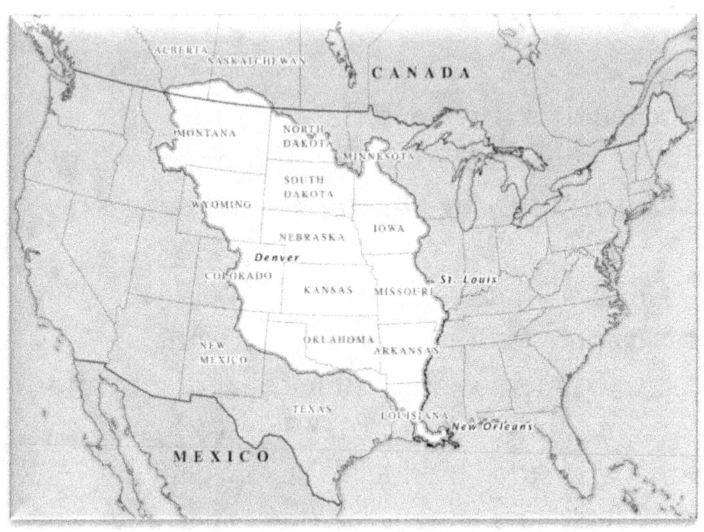

The only hang-up? Nothing in the Constitution authorizes the President, acting on his own, to spend public funds to expand the nation's boundaries. Jefferson knew this perfectly well. The poor guy.

To be fair, it must be noted Jefferson wrestled with this dilemma earnestly, trying to find a legal solution. But time was running out on the deal, so Jefferson caved. He bobbed and he weaved, claiming the President's power to acquire territory was "implied" in the Constitution's clause on treaty-making. Thirteen cents an acre is too good a deal to pass up.

Tricked by a change in the cast of characters: *Talleyrand saved France from the destructive fury of Napoleon's enemies.*

Charles Maurice de Talleyrand (1754 – 1838) was Napoleon Bonaparte's best friend, respected mentor, long-time collaborator, and Foreign Minister. But in 1813, just when Bonaparte stood astride all Europe, having humiliated and conquered every state and nation on the continent, Talleyrand — astute

and far-sighted in a way his master was not —
concluded Napoleon was leading France to ruin
and plotted to bring his master down.

Talleyrand foresaw that Napolean's
conquest of Europe was an "unnatural" state
of affairs totally at odds with the continent's
history. He knew it couldn't last long,
particularly since it was wholly dependent on
the military genius of one man, a soldier who
might well be killed in the battles he was
constantly fighting.

Then in 1813, after his disastrous invasion
of Russia, Bonaparte's fabulous run of luck
ran out. He was fighting a rear-guard action,
trying to make his way back to France,
pursued by the armies of Czar Alexander I,
the Prussian King, and the Emperor of
Austro-Hungary, all hellbent on destruction
and burning for revenge against the French.

It was at this moment Talleyrand struck.
His aim was to protect his beloved homeland
from the destructive rage and retaliation of
Napoleon's conquerors. In effect, he pulled a
rabbit out of his hat.

At this time everyone in Paris was in a
panic and chaos reigned. But Talleyrand, who
never lost his nerve, seized control of events.
He persuaded the hither-to toothless French

Senate to act, establishing a provisional government and making Talleyrand its president. On 2 April, the Senate officially deposed Napoleon; by 11 April, it had adopted a new constitution to re-establish the Bourbon monarchy.

Talleyrand whisked Louis XIII from exile in England and placed him on French throne, a legitimate monarch, the real thing.

When the Allied armies entered Paris in March 1814, Talleyrand greeted them on behalf of His Majesty, King Louis XIII. Surely these crowned heads had no quarrel with their royal "cousin," did they? So, these conquerors, at the head of their armies, should come in peace, should they not? The trick worked. The conquerors now had no excuse to punish France for Napoleon's transgressions. Instead they supped merrily with the French King and his old pal, Talleyrand.

As a result, French cities weren't burned; French civilians weren't slaughtered; French women weren't raped; and French babies weren't bayoneted — which, otherwise, might have been the case. I'd call that a good outcome, wouldn't you? And all thanks to trickery.

Tricked by faith in the U.S. Constitution: *Frederick Douglass genuinely loved America's founding documents -- "all men are created equal"!*

Like most African-Americans of his time, the young Frederick Douglass believed that the failure of the U.S. Constitution to prohibit slavery made it a despicable document. But Douglass, an ardent scholar always, studied the Constitution carefully over time; and as he did, he became convinced the document could be used to support emancipation.

The language of the Constitution, Douglass declared,"contains principles and purposes entirely hostile to the existence of slavery." Indeed, according to Douglass, if these principles and purposes were to be honored, then slavery was *already* unconstitutional.

Frederick Douglass (1818 – 1895) was enslaved in Maryland until 1838 when he escaped to New York City at age 20. He went on to become an American social reformer, orator, writer, statesman, and the greatest abolitionist leader of the 19th century. Here are the highlights of his amazing career.

• In the course of his life, Douglass wrote three autobiographies describing his experiences as a slave. All became bestsellers and were tremendously effective in promoting abolition and racial equality. These books brought Douglass to national prominence. Since then, they have become essential texts of U.S. history.

- He founded a newspaper, *The North Star,* which became the most influential African American antislavery publication of the time.

- Douglass was a brilliant orator, well known for his fiery speeches. His most famous speech is *The Meaning of July Fourth for the Negro*, which he delivered at an event organized by the Rochester Anti-Slavery Sewing Society on July 5, 1852. It is regarded as the greatest anti-slavery oration ever given.

- In 1848, Douglass was the only African American to attend the Seneca Falls Convention, the first women's rights convention held in America. During the convention, Douglass argued passionately in favor of a resolution calling for women's right to vote. The resolution was passed, and a mass social movement demanding women's suffrage was launched.

• During the Civil War (1861–65), Douglass became an advisor to President Lincoln, advocating the arming of former slaves so they could fight for the North. He insisted the war should be fought as an explicit effort to outlaw slavery. Throughout Reconstruction (1865–77), he fought for full civil rights for freedmen.

• In 1877, Douglass was the first African American to be appointed a U.S. marshal. In 1889, he was appointed U.S. minister to Haiti. These appointments were the highest posts given to an African American in 19th century America.

Throughout his long life, Douglass was mocked, insulted, and subjected to violent personal attack. Arsonists burned down his home. But Douglass never flagged in his devotion to the abolitionist cause.

The abolitionists' greatest weapon, Douglass argued, was the Constitution, which he called "a glorious liberty document." He was to declare he "loved" the Constitution.

Douglass loved the Declaration of Independence too, especially the assertion of "self-evident" truths that "all men are created equal" and are born in possession of "inalienable Rights."

In short, Douglass loved America. He loved it for its principles and for its promise. Now, he demanded that white America fully honor the guarantee of natural rights enshrined in the Declaration and the Constitution. And he did not let white America off the hook easily.

As Douglass put it, either all men, regardless of race, were created equal and endowed by their Creator with inalienable rights to life, liberty and the pursuit of happiness — or the Declaration of Independence was a hollow mockery, and America itself was a fraud.

"The existence of slavery in this country brands your republicanism as a sham, your humanity as a base pretense, and your Christianity as a lie," Douglass declared. "It destroys your moral power abroad; it corrupts your politicians at home. It saps the foundation of religion."

Naturally, many white Americans did not welcome hearing this message, southern slaveowners in particular. Slaveowners couldn't bear to see a Black man with such outstanding intellectual capacities. He was a living refutation of their argument that slaves lacked the intellectual capacity to function as independent American citizens.

As I ponder the life and career of Frederick Douglass, it strikes me that his genuine love of liberty and freedom — as defined and enshrined in the Declaration of Independence and the U.S. Constitution — was what drove him forward to great things. He is one of the greatest Americans who ever lived — right up there with Abraham Lincoln. And like Lincoln, he became a world-famous apostle of universal liberty.

Tricked by faith in religion: *In Christianity, Harriet Tubman found the courage to perform miracles.*

Somewhat cynically, American slaveowners compelled their slaves to become Christians, thinking religion would make them more obedient, submissive, and meek. Boy, did this backfire!

Sometimes just the opposite happened. Some slaves embraced the faith so fervently it actually emboldened their efforts to seek freedom. In Christianity, they found the courage needed to do miraculous things.

The star witness here is Harriet Tubman (c. 1820 – 1913) who is the stuff of legend. Tubman was born into slavery in Maryland. She escaped to freedom in the North in 1849 and soon thereafter became a "conductor" on the Underground Railroad, an elaborate secret network of safe houses for runaway slaves. Tubman went into slave territory forty times to rescue and bring back slaves.

It's unclear just how many slaves she rescued, but the number is large, perhaps in the hundreds. Tubman became the most famous "conductor" on the Underground Railroad. She was called "the Moses of her people."

Naturally, Tubman's success brought down on her head the ire of powerful slave owners in the South. Collectively, they put a price on her head. A $40,000 reward was posted for her death or capture (which would be worth over $600,000 today). But — amazingly — Tubman was never captured. She also never lost a "passenger" while leading people to freedom.

If you could ask Harriet Tubman how she managed to pull this off, she'd probably respond by declaring, "Twant me, 'twas the Lord. I always told him, 'I trust to you. I don't know where to go or what to do, but I expect you to lead me,' and He always did."

During the Civil War, Tubman served as a scout, spy, guerrilla soldier, and nurse for the Union Army. She is considered the first African American woman to serve in the military. In her later years, Tubman became an activist in the movement for women's suffrage.

In 2016, in honor of her life, the U.S. Treasury Department announced Tubman will replace Andrew Jackson on the center of a new $20 bill.

Tricked by compassionate conservatism:
British Prime Minister Disraeli persuaded Tories to enact and administer Whig policies and programs.

I'd give my eyeteeth if the ghost of Benjamin Disraeli could be summoned and come roaring back to life as the leader of today's Republican Party.

Dizzy is just the kingpin these misguided wretches desperately need if they are to survive as a political party. He was a political magician for sure, as tricky a shyster that ever came down the pike but, as well, a genuinely compassionate conservative. His speciality was combining rank political opportunism with high moral purpose.

Disraeli (1804 – 1881) was the English wit, novelist, and Tory (conservative) leader who served twice (1868) (1874-1880) as British Prime Minister during the reign of Queen Victoria.

Of the twenty Prime Ministers who served the Queen during her long reign, Dizzy was Victoria's declared favorite. "He is full of poetry, romance, and chivalry," the Queen said of Disraeli. His enemies thought he was full of shit. In truth, he was a shameless flatterer who knew no bounds, especially when addressing the Queen. "Everyone likes flattery," Disraeli said of Victoria, "and when you come to Royalty you should lay it on with a trowel."

Disraeli claimed the key to good government was "Tory men and Whig measures." What he meant by this was things work best when conservatives enact and administer liberal programs and policies. An engaging idea, right? But Disraeli was also playing hard-nosed politics, a game at which he was a master. Basically, he aimed to defeat the Whigs by stealing their ideas and grabbing the credit.

Dizzy called his program *Tory democracy.* This was an unusual blend of political ideas. On the one hand, it advocated preservation of established institutions and traditional principles — all very Tory. On the other, it advocated electoral reform, extending the franchise to working class men. And Tory democracy called for a variety of social and economic reforms designed to benefit common people — all very Whig.

Now, to understand what Dizzy did, and why and how he did it, you need to know something about the times.

In Disraeli's time, England was in the throes of the Industrial Revolution, which created vast new wealth for the upper crust and for the newly flourishing middle class but greatly expanded the gap between them and the working class — then 80% of the population. The mighty force of industrialization herded masses of workers — including many women and children — into early factories where conditions were often filthy and dangerous. There they earned pittances for toiling as long as 16 hours a day, six days a week, with no vacations or holidays.

Moreover, the workers' poor working conditions were matched by equally poor housing and a badly polluted environment — a toxic combination that unleashed outbreaks of diseases such as cholera, typhoid, and typhus.

Disraeli genuinely deplored the dreadful conditions of the working class and feared their consequences. If the ruling elites ignored these conditions (as elites are wont to do), he believed more revolutions would occur, like those that disrupted European social order in 1789, 1830, and 1848. Not surprisingly, this was also at a time when the growing appeal of socialism was posing a threat to the established government.

To rouse his colleagues to act in support of Tory Democracy, Dizzy told them, "Change is inevitable! Change is constant!" Basically (in my words, not his), this is what he told them:

Now, we can stand in the path of this change and be destroyed by its massive force. Or, we can step in and facilitate this change, seeing to it that conservative approaches and methods are employed to smooth the transition, making it both more palatable and more workable.

Besides, we hard-headed Tories know much more about how the world works than the high-minded Whig reformers do, with their lofty ideals and passion for justice.

When it comes to administering needed social change, cool heads are better than warm hearts.

Disraeli was able to persuade his Tory colleagues that working class people — if better housed, fed, and clothed *by* conservatives — would *vote* Conservative. His colleagues bought the pitch. Thus, it was that Disraeli's Tory ministry enacted many liberal measures, including these:

• The Reform Act of 1867, which enfranchised urban male workers for the first time;

• The Agricultural Holdings Act, which addressed tenants' grievances;

• The Artisans Dwellings Act, which mandated slum-clearing and public housing works;

• The Employers and Workmen Act, which made it legal for trade unions to strike;

• The Rivers Pollution Act, which regulated the disposal of waste;

- *The Sale of Food and Drugs Acts, which established standards of safety and purity;

- *The Public Health Act of 1875, which modernized sanitary codes throughout the nation; and

- *The Factory Act, which limited the work hours of women and children.

These reforms delivered solid benefits to the working classes; they even won Disraeli some praise from the opposition. The Liberal-Labour MP Alexander Macdonald told his constituents in 1879, "The Conservative party have done more for the working classes in five years than the Liberals have in fifty." (Macdonald was a Scottish miner who because a trade union leader and one of the first working-class members of the House of Commons.)

Writing from a twentieth-century perspective, Robert Blake, the English historian, declared that Disraeli's ministry constituted "the biggest installment of social reform passed by any one government in the nineteenth century."

Can you imagine any future historian looking back at our time and making a similar observation about today's Republican Party? Of course, you can't. The thought is unthinkable. It would take a dozen Dizzys to reverse the self-destructive course Republicans are now on.

But I can dream, can't I?

Tricked by theatrics: *Was Franklin D. Roosevelt America's greatest actor?*

President Franklin D. Roosevelt (1882 – 1945) was a political magician who could charm the birds out of the trees. In the 1930s, when famed thespian John Barrymore went to the White House to meet the President, Roosevelt greeted him with a wink "What pleasure it is," said Roosevelt, "to meet the second-best actor in America."

Roosevelt might have been serious. Certainly, he is one of the most successful political tricksters of all time. His success was due in large part to his personality. He was charming and funny. He radiated joy and optimism. The people loved and trusted him.

But FDR was not altogether the nice guy he appeared to be. Mostly, it was all an act. Pursuing his objectives, he could be dishonest, guileful, underhanded, even ruthless. In his relationships with others, he could be manipulative, callous, and vindictive — and not warm. "Roosevelt was the coldest man I ever met," Harry Truman said of him.

FDR's deviousness was never more fully employed than after the outbreak of war in Europe in 1939. Roosevelt believed this war would necessarily and inevitably draw in the United States in order to defeat the global reach of Fascism. But first he had to circumvent strong isolationist sentiment in the Congress and in the country. He did so by pretending to maintain American neutrality.

Campaigning in Boston in 1940, he declared, "I have said this before, but I shall say it again, and again and again. Your boys are not going to be sent into any foreign wars." Meanwhile, behind the scenes, FDR was doing all he could to prepare America for entry into the conflict. After Pearl Harbor, FDR went on to lead the nation to victory in the greatest war of all time. As Harry Truman also said of FDR, "He was a great President."

Tricked by unladylike behavior: *Mother Jones put women and children in the front lines of protest marches by striking coalminers.*

Mary G. Harris (1837 – 1930) did not become politically active until she was 50 years old (which was considered elderly in those days). To all appearances, she was a demure, little old lady. But in her post-50 persona as Mother Jones, a fierce labor organizer, Harris was anything but a demure little old lady. Now, she was the greatest woman political agitator of her time, a hell-raiser nonpareil.

Clad in antique black dresses, her face framed by a feminine lace collar and black hat, the five-foot tall Mother Jones was labeled "the most dangerous woman in America" by a U.S. district attorney.

Mother Jones became famous (*infamous?*) as a fearless organizer of coalminers during the first two decades of the 20th century. In this work, she exploited her grandmotherly image to the max, sometimes even exaggerating her age. (How many women are willing to do that? Even for a good cause?)

She would shame mine-workers reluctant to strike, asking them if they'd let themselves be upstaged by a little old woman. "I have been in jail more than once and I expect to go again," she told them. "If you are too cowardly to fight, I will fight for you."

Mother Jones horrified decent people by putting women and children in the front lines of protest marches, which were often attacked violently by goons hired by mine owners to break the marches up. Nothing like this had been done before; and putting innocents at risk was considered a violation of common decency. No lady would do such things. But none of this stopped Mother Jones. She wanted to force people to see the injustice being done to these working families.

Her energy and passion inspired the wives and daughters of miners to join in the fight. She organized miners' wives into teams to guard the mines against scabs (men who'd take the jobs of striking workers). She led a march of workers' wives who chased away strike breakers with mops and brooms.

Mother Jones also worked to abolish child labor. In 1903, she helped organize a "Children's Crusade," a march by 100 or so children who were workers in textile mills. These children marched from the textile mills of Philadelphia to New York City "to show the New York millionaires our grievances."

Along the way, the children would stop in towns to give speeches describing the horror of working conditions in the mills. Many of them were missing limbs as a result of accidents in the mills. Images of these horrors and maiming put the issue of child labor on the top of public agenda, exactly where Mother Jones wanted it to be.

Mary Harris crafted a persona that made her a legend among working people, a legend that persists to this day. (See *Mother Jones*, the magazine.) The creation of this persona may be her greatest achievement.

Most American women in Mother Jones' time led quiet lives, housebound, cooking, cleaning, and caring for their families. Women, especially elderly ones, were not supposed to have opinions. If they did have opinions, they certainly were not expected to voice them publicly. — and certainly not by preaching on street corners.

Let it be said of her: Mother Jones was no lady.

Tricked by sexual innuendo and double entendres: *Mae West launched a worldwide sexual revolution.*

Today, men all over the world are losing power to women, and all over the world, they're freaking out about it. *Boy, are they pissed!* They're demanding answers, explanations! What's *causing* male dominance to wither? Why is it shriveling up?! Why is it drooping like a spent force?! *And who the hell is to blame?!*

These guys are on the prowl, out for blood, tracking down suspects, seeking revenge. Many of them have concluded *liberal democracy* is the cause of male disempowerment — *liberal democracy* with all its newfangled claptrap about "political correctness," women's "lib," and social "justice." To retaliate, these men are fomenting populist revolts that are challenging democracy and the rule of law across the globe.

Speaking as a student of history, I think these guys have gotten off on the wrong foot. They've missed the boat. They attribute *way too much power* to liberal democracy and *way too little* to Mae West.

Truth must be served. If blame is to be placed on the originator of the sexual revolution, it should be placed where it belongs: squarely on the lascivious shoulders of Mae West (1893 – 1980), Hollywood's 1930s screen siren. She's now widely regarded as the precursor of the sexual revolution. Many feminists regard her as its *avatar*.

How did a teensy-weensy girl from
Brooklyn, whose formal education was
limited to dancing lessons, launch a social
revolution that's unprecedented in history?
Well, as it turns out, this blonde bombshell
was packing weapons more potent than even
bee-stung lips, bodacious breasts, and an
hour-glass figure that was the inspiration for
the shape of the Coke bottle. Mae West, it

turns out, had some tricks up the puff sleeves of her sequined gown.

Trick # 1: Mae used *indirection* to deliver a message to women that was perilously subversive. She told them: don't believe what you've been taught! Women are not lesser creatures, dependent on the wisdom and protection of men. *It ain't so!* A woman who looks out for herself can outsmart men and make *them* dependent on *her*. ("Men are like linoleum floors," she declared. "Lay 'em right and you can walk all over them for years.")

Women got the message. During the Depression, they filled movie theaters eager to see this racy, independent woman enjoying life to the fullest without benefit of matrimony. ("Marriage is a great institution," Mae quipped. "But I'm not ready for an institution.")

Trick # 2: Mae used *comedy* to divert males in her audience from the message she was sending women. Men love dirty jokes; Mae loved to tell them. She always left them laughing — laughing so much, in fact, they failed to notice *they* were the butt of the jokes. ("A hard man is good to find," she observed.)

Mae had no fear of male audiences, not even raucous ones. She held them in the palm of her hand. As a young actress, she'd honed her performance skills working on the burlesque circuit playing before predominantly male working-class audiences. ("I know so much about men," she said, "because I went to night school.")

Trick # 3: In her movies, Mae turns the tables on men by *behaving like one*. She's the sexually provocative protagonist. She chooses, uses, and discards male sex partners on a whim. She takes command; she's in charge; and she never surrenders a bit of freedom or control.

(In her 1933 film, *She Done Him Wrong*, West's co-star is the young, dazzlingly handsome Cary Grant, who portrays a virtuous temperance league member. Intrigued, Mae looks him over from head to toe, sizes him up, and delivers her verdict, "You can be had.")

Trick # 4: In Mae's movies, the scarlet woman she portrays is *not* punished for her sins — a blatant violation of society's prudish moral code. Instead, her movies always have a happy ending when the sexually rebellious heroine triumphs over a censorious society. ("I believe in censorship," Mae joked. "I made a fortune out of it.")

Tricks # 5: In her movies, Mae West plays — there's no other way to put it — a *drag queen*. Except in her case she's a woman "dragging" her own gender. But like male drag queens, she's a sexual transgressor who protests and defies gender norms that compel males and females to behave in strictly prescribed ways based on their sexual organs.

Mae lampoons femininity every bit as much as she lampoons masculinity. Her screen persona is a grossly exaggerated image of femininity. Look at her! See the the hour-glass figure encased in a corset so tight she could scarcely breathe. See her tottering on shoes with heels so high (nine and one-half inches) she can scarcely walk! It's a burlesque of conventional ideas of womanly appeal.

But here's the thing: Mae's exaggerated femininity is a comic performance. Actually, she's *mocking* the rituals of mating. So, she's not a *real* sex symbol, she's a *parody* of one.

Mae — bless her heart!— is saying gender isn't that big a deal. She puts gender in its place, not as the most important determinant of our identity, but only as one aspect of it. More importantly, she exposes the *artificiality* of gender, not as something *natural* but as a *cultural* concept. *Wow!* This is mind blowing!

Mae West sees gender as something contrived by a conformist society that's determined to repress human sexual malleability. She sees gender as a penal system in which people are sentenced for life, men in one prison and women in another. Mae wants us all to break out of prison and go have some fun. If that isn't a good excuse for a social revolution, I don't know what is.

Tricked by the use of a demigod as a bargaining chip: *How General Douglas MacArthur managed to establish democracy in postwar Japan.*

"If you want to test a man's character," the adage goes, "give him power."

The character of General Douglas MacArthur (1880 – 1964) has been much tested and found wanting. He was a deeply flawed man — self-centered, egocentric, and vain to the extreme. He compared himself to Alexander the Great, Caesar, and Napoleon and thought he excelled them all. Like his contemporary, the French general, Charles de Gaulle (whom we shall encounter shortly), he was so aloof and autocratic he drove his underlings bonkers.

But MacArthur possessed great strengths too. He had a powerful intellect, magnificent courage, great presence of mind, and boundless energy in action. The general loved to work and got immense satisfaction from doing it well. And his grasp of military strategy was brilliant, second to none.

After Japan's defeat in World War II, MacArthur was given power — great power. *And this time his character would not be found wanting.*

In August 1945, President Truman appointed MacArthur Supreme Commander for the Allied Powers, which gave him command of all Allied Forces in Japan. MacArthur became, in effect, the defeated nation's American viceroy, exercising vast power over the ruined country's occupation and rebuilding.

His task was Herculean. It was nothing less than to install a new political order in Japan, one based on individual rights, democracy, and the rule of law. This represented a revolutionary departure from the historical experience of the Japanese that had been, in essence, feudal.

The old boy pulled this task off and in spades too! During his viceroyship (1945 – 1951), he demobilized Japan's military forces, purged right-wing militarists, and restored the economy. Most importantly, he oversaw the crafting and adoption of a liberal constitution that introduced significant reforms in land redistribution, education, labor, public health, and women's rights. (The wags had a field day, joking that MacArthur had succeeded in establishing Roosevelt's New Deal in Japan.)

MacArthur's achievement is all the more impressive when you consider how dreadful conditions were in postwar Japan. Chaos reigned. Over two million people had been killed. All the large cities, the industries, and the transportation systems were in ruins. Many people were homeless. Famine was widespread, and the country was almost entirely out of rice, its staple food.

Moreover, with the Japanese masses in such distress, MacArthur had to contend with the possibility of a communist takeover. Communist agitators, backed by Moscow, were all over the place. And in nearby China, a Communist revolution was sweeping to victory.

If that weren't enough, there was the stirrings of a coup by right-wing militarists who refused to accept Japan's defeat and were determined to fight on.

In this national collapse, one factor remained clear and constant: the veneration the Japanese felt for the Emperor. According to Japanese tradition, Emperor Hirohito was a direct descendant of Amaterasu, the Sun Goddess, and thus was a deity rather than an ordinary human being.

So, while the nation was subjected to the pain and humiliation of defeat, none of this shame touched the monarchy. In the eyes of the Japanese people, the Emperor remained unblemished, inviolable, the sacrosanct emblem that held the country together.

This mystical bond did not escape the attention of Douglas MacArthur. Not much of strategic importance did. His job was to pacify the Japanese people and to bring them into *willing* cooperation with his plans for a revolutionary new political order. In a coldly arrived at strategic calculation, General MacArthur decided to use the Emperor's continued existence as a bargaining chip. The game was on!

Back in Washington many powerful figures were demanding the Emperor be deposed, tried as a war criminal, and hanged. Most of the senior military brass were clamoring for the same thing. At the same time, the British, Russians, Australians, Koreans, and Chinese were all pressing President Truman to charge Hirohito with war crimes.

A resolution passed by the Senate instructed MacArthur to "proceed immediately to assemble all available evidence of Hirohito's participation in and responsibility for Japanese violations of international law." The Joint Chiefs of Staff sent MacArthur a similar instruction.

MacArthur, however, was convinced the preservation of Emperor was vital for Japan's stability and for bringing about the democratic changes to the country he was planning. Plus, he knew that to dethrone or hang the Emperor would cause tremendous and violent reaction from masses of Japanese people.

MacArthur was a stubborn man, determined to get his own way when he knew he was right. And he was not afraid to be insubordinate. On his own, he decided to spare the Emperor Hirohito from charges as a war criminal. The entire Japanese nation breathed a sigh of relief.

For his part, Hirohito — mindful of the gallows — did what he had to do. He issued a public declaration renouncing his semi-divine status and declaring he was, like his subjects, merely human. (Not a word of this statement — which was only two paragraphs long — was written by the Son of Heaven. It was written in its entirety by the Administrative Assistant to the heaven-sent General MacArthur.)

As noted earlier, MacArthur oversaw the drafting of a new constitution in which he allowed the emperor to remain as head of state, thereby assuaging Japanese pride and restoring social order.

Since Japanese law stipulated that only the emperor had the authority to revise Japan's constitution, Hirohito was called upon to do so. He promulgated the new constitution on November 3, 1946, and the Japanese people willingly accepted it as legitimate. Universal suffrage was established, including votes for women. Labor was given the right to organize.

All this paid off handsomely. MacArthur's viceroyship led to the most peaceful and prosperous era in Japanese history. Ten years after his departure, Japan emerged as the world's second largest economy, enjoying national prosperity and social stability.

Tricked by simplicity: *Gandhi as a political showman.*

Mohandas Gandhi (1869 – 1948) was the leader and hero of India's struggle to win the independence from Great Britain. He is perhaps the most revered figure in India's history. Millions of his fellow Indians extol Gandhi as a "Mahatma," or "great soul," one of the most righteous and venerable of men.

Speaking in Madison Avenue terms, if I may, I'd say being hailed as a "Mahatma" is about the best publicity a politician can get. *What can top it?* Holy cow, I'll bet there are hundreds of politicians — on the left *and* right — who'd sell their souls to be called Mahatma. Bill Clinton for one. And Donald Trump for sure. But — let's face it — there's only *one* Mahatma, and that's Mahatma *Gandhi.*

Now I know Gandhi never held political office. I know many people see him as saintly — far too pure and high-minded to engage in the grubby business of politics. But that's not how I see him.

I see Gandhi as a shrewd political operator who weighed every action and word in a calculated manner. In fact, in my book, he's one of the canniest political tricksters who ever lived. *And a good thing too!* That's how he managed to win dominion status for his beloved homeland.

As a lone individual challenging the greatest empire on earth, Gandhi possessed a great advantage: *he believed his own publicity.*

He had a sense of mission so strong it amounted to a form of moral egotism. He felt called to leadership; and, moreover, he felt he was indispensable to the great task at hand. This unshakable belief in himself was strong enough to convince many fellow Indians that Gandhi, a man dwelling amongst them, was a living saint.

Gandhi was not a living saint; no flesh-and-blood mortal can be. Perhaps I should note here the Mahatma has many critics and stands accused of many flaws, but none of that bothers me at all. I'm not looking for nonexistent living saints, I'm looking for living, breathing politicians who employed deviousness to get the right thing done. And Gandhi sure fits the bill.

His motif was simplicity. Gandhi was hailed as the ultimate messiah for the poor, because he himself chose to live in abject poverty so he could understand their pain. But this image was contrived in many ways.

Sarojini Naidu, President of the Indian National Congress, his friend and ardent supporter, once jokingly observed, "It costs a lot of money to keep this man in poverty." She knew maintaining Gandhi's sizable retinue was costly.

Gandhi brimmed with contradictions.

He denounced modern conveniences, but he made full use of the trappings of modern civilization. For instance, sophisticated press and media operations characterized all his campaigns.

He opposed industrialization but sought useful alliances with Indian industrialists. His campaigns were made possible by financial contributions from rich patrons.

Gandhi preferred to live in a hut, but his huts were somewhat special. Before he moved into one, his team visited it in advance. They renovated and strengthened the hut with concrete, and they sanitized and whitewashed the walls. The hut was outfitted with electricity and a telephone.

Similarly, whenever Gandhi travelled, he insisted on traveling third class, uncomfortably crowded with poor people. But his backup team was understandably concerned about his security (there were frequent attempts to assassinate him). So, they booked an entire compartment in

advance, filled it with Gandhi supporters
dressed in soiled clothes, pretending to be
poor passengers.

The press ate it up. Whenever Gandhi
boarded a train, embraced and cheered on by
gaggles of the poor, the cameras were there to
capture the image and transmit it all over the
world.

The world paid heed.

I argue that it takes nothing away from
Gandhi's spiritual and religious significance
to show what a clever operator he was. Look
at what he accomplished. He pitted his
person, his body, and his personal lifestyle
against the might of the British Empire, and
he won.

Tricked by grandeur: *Charles de Gaulle as a
political showman.*

Earlier, in the opening of this part of the
book, I described Charles de Gaulle's strange,
but entirely earnest, belief that he incarnated
France — embodying in his person elements

of Joan of Arc, Louis XIV, and Napoleon Bonaparte. And I noted this conviction of his was so evident and so strong that many French people *believed it too*. I concluded by reporting that this conviction helped de Gaulle win election to the French Presidency in 1959. Quite a story, huh?

Here's the end of it. General de Gaulle was called to the Presidency to extricate France from a disastrous and hopeless mess. France was then engaged in a long and terrible war with Algeria, its rebellious colony in North Africa. By 1959, the Algerian War had frozen public opinion between those who were determined to hang on to the colony and those who were willing to grant it independence. It looked like the country was on the brink of army revolt or civil war.

This mess was gravely complicated.

France was tied to Algeria through the presence of one million European settlers, who saw themselves as French. They were united by an attachment to the privileged status that French control over Algeria gave them. They owned the colony's best land and filled all the best jobs.

They had a powerful lobby in Paris, through which they controlled, in effect, the appointed colonial government.

As you might expect, these Europeans were heartily despised by Algeria's nine million Muslim majority, who always got the short end of the stick. Tensions between the two population groups came to a head in 1954, when the first violent events kicked off what was to become the Algerian War.

In May 1958, the crisis intensified when European Algerians launched massive demonstrations calling for the integration of Algeria into France proper. To ensure this outcome, the rebels demanded that Charles de Gaulle, their hero, be called to power.

This move was supported by right-wing nationalists and by militarists in the French Army who were certain de Gaulle, as the self-identified embodiment of French grandeur, would support the retention of Algeria and its incorporation into France. And they were certain his mystical bond with the French people would work its magic.

The outcome would be a larger and a *grander* France.

These boys were in for a surprise.

Privately, de Gaulle had concluded the Age of Colonization had ended and that granting Algeria its independence was the only option France had left. So, once he secured the Presidency, de Gaulle ended the Algerian War, withdrew the French from Algeria, and gave Algeria its independence. In doing this, de Gaulle betrayed some of his most devoted supporters on the right. (Many never forgave him. They kept plotting his assassination; there were at least 30 attempts to kill him.)

The right-wingers were right about one thing, however: de Gaulle's mystical bond with the French people did indeed work its magic.

On April 22, 1961, a group of French generals attempted a coup d'etat intended to force President de Gaulle not to abandon Algeria. The following day, de Gaulle made a famous speech on television, imploring the French people and military to help him defeat the coup. Ever the trickster, de Gaulle appeared on screen dressed in his old World War II uniform, a forceful sentimental tug on the hearts of his audience and a vivid reminder of his wartime heroism. The speech — and maybe the uniform — did the trick. The coup collapsed immediately.

Here's the thing: de Gaulle's exalted image of himself reflected his exalted image of France. He conceived of France as being on what he called a "civilizing mission," setting standards for the rest of the world. Compared to the rest of the world, France's civilization is superior — humane, wise, tolerant, generous, and farsighted.

Now, as it happens, the French are quite fond of seeing themselves as bearers of a "civilizing mission," setting standards for the rest of the world. In this, the French people and de Gaulle were on the same page, and de Gaulle knew it perfectly well.

Now, it was this wise, enlightened France that would graciously extend independence to the Algerians. And so it happened.

I must say I get a kick out of this story, especially given this book's premise about the potency of benevolent trickery. In my jolly and idiosyncratic way, I see this: The conflict pitted de Gaulle and his inflated and semi-delusional image of himself against the political and military might of right-wing nationalists and militarists. *And de Gaulle's inflated and semi-delusional image of himself won!*

For all his vanity, arrogance, and many deplorable flaws, Charles de Gaulle occupies an honorable place in history. When he was called to power in 1958, he got France out of the Algerian mess, and he saved his nation from civil war. Most importantly, de Gaulle brought stability to France by installing a viable new constitution. His Fifth Republic survives to this day.

Tricked by mumbling: *Dwight Eisenhower deliberately concealed his strengths so his foes would underestimate him.*

Throughout his long military career, Dwight ("Ike") Eisenhower (1890 – 1969) made a practice of concealing his strengths so his foes would underestimate him. He didn't mind being thought a lightweight so long as he got his way, as often he did.

Many historians regard Eisenhower as the most successful general of the Second World War. Certainly, he was the only American President in the 20th century to preside over eight years of peace and prosperity.

Furthermore, as President, he guided the free world through the 1950s — one of the most dangerous decades of the Cold War.

During his Presidency, however, many people critical of him lampooned him as a doddering old man who was not up to the job. Hearing his often meandering and garbled answers to questions put to him at White House press conferences, the era's pundits wondered aloud if Ike still had all his marbles.

It turns out the joke was on the critics and the pundits. Ike *tricked* them and a lot of other people besides.

By the time he reached the White House, Ike had perfected a variety of techniques for concealing his strengths. He was especially good at mumbling answers to questions put to him by the press. But behind the apparent incoherence was a brilliant intellectual tactician playing a subtle game.

Remember, Ike was a guy who crossed verbal swords, at one time or another, with Franklin Roosevelt, General Patton, Winston

Churchill, Field Marshal Montgomery, Joseph Stalin, and Charles de Gaulle. And, remember too, in these disputes, Ike seldom, if ever, came out on the losing side.

(It's worth noting that Ike was the only one of the Allied leaders who forged a decent working relationship with de Gaulle, who was the most difficult man to deal with on the face of the earth.)

Eisenhower was a master of calculated duplicity, and he used his skills to confuse the Soviet, Chinese, and other foreign foes. *They did not know what to make of him. What was he thinking? What were his plans?* Meanwhile, Eisenhower, behind the scenes, assiduously deployed his actual many strengths to guide policy in the direction he wanted.

Richard Nixon described the President under whom he served as Vice President for eight years as "by far the most devious man I ever met in my life." (And, yes, it takes one to know one.)

The 1950s were the height of the Cold War; and, throughout the decade, dangerous provocations brought great pressure on President Eisenhower to respond militarily. His foreign policy and military advisers, for example, wanted to use the atom bomb to stem an expanding communist threat in Indochina. Ike, the war hero, refused, mumbling all the way. By keeping his enemies confused at all times, he made sure no wars were fought on his watch.

Tricked by a tiger changing its stripes (#2): Lyndon Johnson, a southern racist, became the greatest civil rights President since Abraham Lincoln.

I have long retained a vivid recollection of Ladybird Johnson making an appearance on television at the 1960 Democratic National Convention in Los Angeles. She was alone onscreen, outside the Convention Hall, speaking just after her husband, Lyndon, had lost his bid for the Presidential nomination to John F. Kennedy.

Mrs. Johnson was sad, of course, even mournful. But she spoke with such dignity and conviction I was deeply impressed. I

don't remember her exact words, but here is
the gist of it:

*Most people don't know it, but Lyndon has a
huge heart and a great, generous spirit. If he is
ever given the chance, he is capable of doing
tremendous good for the country.*

I didn't know it then — and as a stalwart
young liberal, I wouldn't have believed it —
but the day would come when I was to realize
Mrs. Johnson was absolutely right about her
husband's capacity to do great things.

In 1960, I thought Lyndon Johnson was a
southern racist, and I wasn't far off base.

In the 1950s, as the all-powerful majority
leader of the United States Senate, LBJ was
second only to President Eisenhower in
national power and influence. Much of
Johnson's power derived from his position as
leader of the Senate's Southern bloc. As such,
he worked hard to stonewall civil rights
legislation. And he wasn't polite about it.

Johnson was a notorious vulgarian who
constantly used the N-word. He often

behaved in ways that were boorish and bullying. What a strange mixture he was. A longtime aide described LBJ as someone who could be "cruel and kind, generous and greedy, sensitive and insensitive, crafty and naive, ruthless and thoughtful, simple in many ways yet extremely complex, caring and totally not caring."

So how did Lyndon Johnson become a civil rights hero who is lauded to this day? The answer is that he yearned to be lauded, and he yearned to do good.

Ladybird and others who were close to him believed LBJ also felt genuine compassion for African Americans, for the poor, and for the disadvantaged. He spoke often of the hardships of his own childhood, and those memories seemed to inspire him to achieve something significant with his life if he got the chance.

The event that changed everything was, of course, the assassination of President Kennedy. The overwhelming public response to JFK's assassination gave his successor a rare opportunity for combining political

opportunism with high moral purpose. LBJ
made the most of it.

Using all his powers to the utmost, he
forcibly secured passage of the Civil Rights
Act of 1964 and Voting Rights Act of 1965 —
two of the most consequential laws ever
passed by Congress.

Robert Caro, LBJ's great biographer,
explains his conduct in this way:

"He always had this true, deep compassion
to help poor people and particularly poor
people of color, but even stronger than the

compassion was his ambition. But when the two aligned, when compassion and ambition finally are pointing in the same direction, then Lyndon Johnson becomes a force for racial justice, unequalled certainly since Lincoln."

Tricked by a tiger changing its stripes (# 3): *Nixon went to China.*

If the daughters of Richard Nixon ever asked him, "What did you do in the war, Daddy?" he might have answered, "I made enough money playing poker to pay for my first run for Congress."

That's true, he did.

Despite being raised a Quaker and being taught gambling was a sin, Nixon became a cracker jack poker player when he was serving in the Navy during World War II. He knew nothing about the game when he started, and he didn't play it for pleasure, far from it. He was a young man who needed money to chase his ambitions; and stuck in a war in the midst of the Pacific, winning poker games was about the only option he had.

Once he determined his goal, Nixon pursued it with the utmost seriousness. Before beginning to play, he studied the game intensively. He interviewed mates who were good players and quizzed them exhaustively. He was a quick learner, and all his effort paid off big time.

At the time Nixon, as a lieutenant in the Naval Reserve, was earning $150 a month. But — *zounds!* — in a few months he managed to earn over $7,000 playing poker. *That's equivalent to $100,000 today.* The money was soon to be used to fund Nixon's first —and successful — run for Congress in 1946.

Looking back, we can see this wartime episode as an early demonstration of Nixon's strengths, including his massive capacity for hard work. He calculated the odds coldly and realistically. He showed courage and daring. Nixon became known as a player who was exceptionally good at bluffing and at assessing and taking risks. He was "Tricky Dick" way back then.

This brings us to China, or, speaking more precisely it brings us to the phrase, "Nixon goes to China." This phrase has become part of our political lexicon. It means a moment in which a leader reverses his past positions to do something that is shocking but beneficial.

As President, Nixon secretly initiated negotiations with China. He knew the Soviet Union and Red China, despite their facade of ideological unity, were actually in deep conflict. So, Nixon's strategy was to play off one against the other. Ultimately Nixon visited China and broke bread with Mao Zedong.

Nixon's trip to China ended twenty-five years of isolation between the United States and the People's Republic of China and resulted in establishment of diplomatic relations between the two countries in 1979.

Given his lifelong reputation as a fierce anti-communist ideologue, Nixon could risk such a gigantic flip-flop in foreign policy, something no dovish Democratic President could afford to do politically.

Now, obviously, Richard Nixon is no role model for a democratic leader. His deviousness was to be employed for dark purposes. "Tricky Dick" encouraged illegal actions by his subordinates. But here I salute his daring to be inconsistent and his willingness to jettison the past in favor of something fresh and new.

Nixon's trip to China is remembered today as a remarkable act of brave leadership. He took a big risk. The whole thing could have blown up in his face. But the old card shark played his hand well and the whole world benefited.

Tricked by ladylike demeanor: *How Mrs. Ronald Reagan ended the Cold War without firing a shot.*

The Patriarchal Code specifies that a good political wife, making public appearances with her hubby, should stand by her man's side, dutifully gazing up at him adoringly.

In this category, Mrs. Ronald Reagan established the world's standard. No First Lady ever appeared more prim or proper. Always impeccably dressed and coiffed, Mrs. Reagan was usually viewed as a "traditional" first lady — mostly interested in fashion, White House interior design, entertaining guests, and planning State Dinners.

But no First Lady was ever a greater behind-the-scenes force in the White House. In private, she was unafraid to speak her mind to the President and to key White House officials about the goings-on in her husband's administration.

Reagan was a hawk; his wife was a dove.

Ken Duberstein, a former chief of staff for Ronald Reagan, remembers Nancy Reagan as someone who truly believed "the art of governing required compromise" and relied upon relationship building.

First ladies can also be vital players in diplomatic relations, and Nancy Reagan certainly was. Her rapport with Mikhail and Raisa Gorbachev was essential to nurturing the warm and productive relationship that the President developed with the Soviet leader between 1985 and 1988.

Mrs. Reagan waded into foreign policy, siding with and aiding moderate voices within the administration that wanted Ronald Reagan to negotiate with the Soviet Union in their battle against hawks in the Administration who opposed the idea.

During the negotiations, she aggressively pushed back against more conservative advisers and politicians who were warning the President that this was a mistake

Their meetings led to several arms limitation deals, a remarkable friendship between a lifetime anti-communist and lifelong communist, and the eventual end of the Cold War and the breakup of the Soviet Union. And all without firing a shot.

Mrs. Reagan never upstaged her husband or took credit for these accomplishments. Of course, in obedience to the Patriarchal Code, no male leader can openly acknowledge his wife's contribution. This is true even of

Ronald Reagan, whose missus was his only close confidant and his primary political adviser — an open secret every political observer in America knew.

Nevertheless, in 1987, near the end of his Administration, President Reagan, speaking of his wife, declared, "The idea that she is involved in governmental decisions and so forth and all of this, there is nothing to that." Reagan called this view of his wife "despicable fiction."

(Oh, by the way, Mrs. Reagan had a first name. It was Nancy.)

Tricked by pop culture: *Ellen DeGeneres and gay rights advocates built public support for same-sex marriage by scorning conventional politics.*

When Congress passed the Defense of Marriage Act in 1996, same-sex marriage was not legal *anywhere* in the United States. And the door to political acceptance of same-sex unions had been not only firmly *slammed* shut but *nailed* shut too. Thirty-one states had actually passed *constitutional* amendments banning legal recognition of same-sex unions. Yet, in 2015, the U.S. Supreme Court legalized same-sex marriage in all fifty states.

What a triumph for social progress! And unforeseen too! How did it happen?

Here's my take on it. Between 1996 and 2015, a tremendous shift in public opinion took place. As I witnessed it, gay rights advocates "stole the march" on political intolerance by using *pop culture* to build public support for gay marriage.

Today, some politically savvy social critics argue that pop culture is *more powerful than politics.* To me, that's a breathtaking assertion! What's more, given the present deplorable — even hopeless — state of politics in America, I yearn for the assertion to be sound. We *need* a backdoor to social progress. Pop culture may be it. So what the hell is it anyway?

Pop culture is the sum total of the thoughts, ideas, attitudes, perspectives, and images that the mainstream population prefers. (This preference is especially marked among young people.) And pop culture takes many forms: music, television, movies, video games, fashion, sports, news, slang, and, of course, comedy.

Which brings me to Ellen.

In 1996, the Defense of Marriage Act became law. One year later, Ellen DeGeneres — famous comedian and TV star — decided to "come out" on her sitcom. Her daring came at a cost. Ellen was condemned by the religious right, and some sponsors pulled their advertising from her TV show, but — on the other hand — she landed on the cover of *Time* magazine.

I think DeGeneres probably did more to influence Americans' attitudes about gay rights than any other celebrity or public figure. Perhaps it's no accident that it was a comedian who served as an agent for same-sex marriage in the public debate. Comedians are like jesters at royal courts who were allowed to get away with murder so long as they were funny.

Of course, Ellen wasn't the only court jester. Other openly gay comics — Rosie O'Donnell for example — and satirical TV sitcoms with witty homosexual characters — *Fame, Will & Grace, Modern Family* — made America laugh too, all the while they were delivering a gay rights message.

I argue that, in the dramatic struggle over same-sex unions, comedy and satire played outsized parts. Why? Because the primary foe of gay rights is the *patriarchy* and among the patriarchy's many unappealing characteristics is *humorlessness*.

This makes the old boys a particularly fit subject for ridicule and caricature. Ridicule and caricature are *themselves* a potent form of politics, and — get this — *the old boys don't know how to defend themselves from it.* They're babes in the woods, easy prey.

Here's the icing on the cake: gays are masters of the medium. They toss jokes and jibes around like jugglers. And when it comes to their own defense, they toss *daggers*. Ask any drag queen of your acquaintance, and she'll gladly explain it to you.

When it comes to pop culture, the patriarchs don't know their asses from a hole in the ground. Pop culture *confounds* them; it *unnerves* them. So when confronted with massive public support for same sex unions, the hierarchy of patriarchy trembled, shook, and fell.

I contend *to this day* the patriarchy still doesn't know what hit it.

Tricked by Youth: Fifteen-year-old Greta Thunberg asks world leaders a simple question and, in doing so, exposes the fallacy of economics.

What magic does Greta Thunberg possess that has swiftly transported the obscure Swedish teenager onto the world stage? Is it her ability to ask world leaders simple, direct questions that stump them?

In the summer of 2018, Greta, then a 15-year-old Swedish girl, started demonstrating outside the Swedish parliament every Friday as part of what she called "a climate strike." When she started, she was demonstrating solo; but, remarkably, she soon became the face of a worldwide movement by young people demanding stronger action on climate change.

On September 20, 2019, Thunberg led the largest "climate strike" in history. Millions of students all over the world walked out of school to engage in day-long climate protests. These strikes were so compelling world leaders couldn't ignore them, however much they may have wanted to.

As a result, Thunberg — viewed as spokesperson for these masses of young people — was invited to address the United Nations, the US Congress, UK Parliament, and various international conferences on climate change. Pretty heady stuff for a teenaged girl, but none of this daunted her.

In these speeches, Thunberg blasted world leaders for their "empty words and promises which give the impression that sufficient action is being taken." She asked them, "what will you tell your children was the reason you failed and left them facing the climate chaos you knowingly brought upon them?"

Not surprisingly, world leaders were peeved by these attacks, especially since Greta's every utterance was instantly broadcast by worldwide media.

Most notably, she clashed with US Treasury Secretary Steven Mnuchin at the 2020 meeting of the World Economic Forum, the annual schmooze-fest that brings billionaires and world leaders to "network" with one another in Davos, a Swiss ski resort.

(Mnuchin, it should be noted, is the very embodiment of a white male elitist, born with a silver spoon in his mouth. Naturally, he got an Ivy League education, graduating from Yale in 1985 with a bachelor's degree in economics. Skull and Bones? You betcha! Next, right on target, Mnuchin made a trek to Wall Street where he effortlessly climbed the ladder of success, privilege by privilege. Eventually, he became Executive Vice President of Goldman Sachs, one of the largest investment banking enterprises in the world. When Mnuchin left the company in 2002, he took an estimated $46 million of company stock with him.)

At the Davos meeting, Mnuchin sharply criticized the financial credentials of the 17-year-old girl (who had then not graduated from high school). He said she should go to college and study economics before weighing in on policy. "Greta Thunberg can tell us what to do after she goes and studies economics in college," Mnuchin declared.

Greta's response was remarkably short and simple. "All I'm asking," she said, "is that you put your children first."

Now — here — I must pause and take a deep breath. *Whew!*

As I see things, Greta's response to Secretary Mnuchin knocked the ball out of the park! In one fell swoop, she nailed him to the wall! That's because the Treasury Secretary is at a disadvantage here. The poor dope actually believes that *economics* is more important than *children*.

Greta knows better. She knows that — for all humanity — the most important thing by far is *love of children.* Knowing this, she can run rings around Secretary Mnuchin and, for that matter, the entire discipline of economics.

Here's what it boils down to: *economists can't put children first. They don't know how!*

Here is what incapacitates them.

Economists are slaves to quantification. They grovel before its alter. If a thing can't be counted, it doesn't exist. But, as Einstein observed, "Not everything that counts can be counted, and not everything that can be counted counts." Included here are such essential, life-affirming qualities as cooperation, sharing, unpaid caring for others, and volunteering. And, surely, the nurture of children tops this list. Try putting an economic value on that!

Its practitioners like to claim economics is a science, on a par with — say — chemistry, medicine, or physics. Not so, says Hazel Henderson, the renowned futurist who is one of the world's leading experts on sustainable development. Henderson dismisses economics as a pseudo-science.

"The theories of economists are largely unprovable hypotheses — quite different from those in the hard sciences, which can be empirically verified or refuted," Henderson declares. "For example, the equations which guide spaceships to the moon or in constructing a bridge must be correct. Or the bridge will collapse and the spaceship self-destruct. But economists' so-called principles are mere concepts, which often conceal political or social ideologies behind smokescreens of fancy mathematics."

I think Hazel Henderson is absolutely on the mark when she exposes economics as a disguised form of politics — an insight which prompts me to ask: *what then is the function of economics in politics?* Well, in this particular case, I'd say the function of economics is to say, "No, you *can't* put children first! It's not permitted. We can't afford it."

So, I say to Secretary Mnuchin, there's no need for Greta to learn economics. The need is for you to *unlearn* it.

POSTLUDE

Plato hated democracy, and Socrates didn't much like it either. It must be said both men knew what they were talking about. Both had seen Athenian democracy close up and knew what a rickety affair it was.

Plato saw democracies as anarchic societies, which lacked the internal unity essential for social order and the survival of the state. Democracies, he said, were guided much too much by the caprices of the crowd when they ought to be guided by a pursuit of the common good.

Plato portrayed Socrates as deeply pessimistic about democracy.

Socrates believed voting in an election was a solemn responsibility that required some skill to perform. He thought people should be taught this skill. They should *know something* about what they're voting on.

Letting them vote without an education is irresponsible, dangerous, and leads to power grabs by demagogues. Socrates knew all too well how easy it is for ambitious, ruthless politicians to exploit the public's gullibility and cluelessness.

Alas, the flaws in democracy identified by Plato and Socrates proved to be fatal in their day. Athenian democracy was short-lived. It *did* crash and burn for the very reasons they outlined.

Now, I don't suppose it will shock many readers to hear — now, over two thousand years later — these salient warnings are as germane as they were in ancient Athens.

Assaults on democracy and the rule of law are now endemic. The common good is being exploited and destroyed along with the natural environment on which it rests. And in both cases, flaws in democracy have enflamed the problem while impeding remedial action. Holy cow; can things get any crummier?!

It's in this dread context that I've written this book about how to trick people into doing the right thing. (And — by the way — I had a jolly good time writing it too! Seeing the bad guys pulling *dirty* tricks being confounded by the good guys pulling *clean* tricks is a cure for whatever ails you.)

Mind you, everything I've reported here is *frigging* true. I am not jesting! Scoff if you want, but it's *true* the Cold War may not have ended as it did without the backstairs management of Nancy Reagan, a mere woman who held no public office or official power. In history, that's the way the cookie crumbles.

Here's the thing: *benevolent trickery circumvents the flaws in democracy.* So it's no trivial thing! It is no sideshow in history. It is front and center. *Jumping Jehoshaphat, benevolent trickery provides many of the high points in history.* Ponder these:

• Benevolent trickery is what enabled Pericles to fashion the glory that was Greece. It's what enabled Augustus to inaugurate the Pax Romana,

• Benevolent trickery is what enabled Ben Franklin to persuade the French to fund the American Revolution, thereby making its victory possible. It's what enabled Abe Lincoln to free the slaves.

• Benevolent trickery is what enabled Mae West to launch a worldwide sexual revolution that has subverted the three-thousand-year-old patriarchy. It's what enabled gay rights advocates to achieve the unthinkable: the legalization of same-sex marriage.

Wow, that's some record! And it's just a few of the highlights. (If I wanted to, I could write a couple more books about benevolent trickery. In this one, I just scratched the surface.)

Now, we must ask: is benevolent trickery up to the challenges before us in these messiest of moments? Just now, these calamities are noisily kicking in the front as well as the back door.

Well, I certainly hope deviousness will continue to save our asses from the punishment our misbehavior seems to call for, but I cannot speak with any certainty about this. The answer, when it comes, will come in the form of surprises.

I'll be honest. Here's what I'm counting on.

I'm counting on a bountiful nature to keep supplying us with gifted, shrewd, political leaders, and daring civic dissenters who will be good enough liars and good enough actors to carry on the tradition of Queen Elizabeth I, President Franklin Roosevelt, Mahatma Gandhi, and the other grand tricksters profiled in this book.

If all else fails, in the end, like the late, great Frederick Douglass, I place my faith in the hope and promise of liberty and freedom enshrined in nation's founding documents by America's Founding Fathers. Even with all that's gone wrong, they're still the best bets we've got.

How to Trick People into Doing the Right Thing

APOLOGIES

As an 82-year-old white male American who's been a passionate history buff all my life, I've read thousands of biographies of political figures, nearly all of them *about* white men, and nearly all of them *written* by white men.

Don't condemn me! What the hell else was I going to read?! I grew up as a working-class boy in a small town in Ohio. For a boy of my time and place, white male history was *all the history there was.*

Okay, all this is changing now, and I couldn't be more welcoming. Hey, I'm a gay man! I know a thing or two about being marginalized in the history books.

Reading as a young man, however voraciously, I wouldn't have encountered any suggestion that gay people even existed. If I read a biography of Frederick the Great (as I did), it never would have intimated in any way he was homosexual. If I read a biography of Florence Nightingale (as I did), it never would have intimated in any way that she was a Lesbian.

Where I really fall down is here: nearly all my reading has been in *Western* history. I know next to nothing about Asian or African history. I know a bit, but not much, about Latin-American history.

In my defense, I will say in writing this book I've endeavored to compensate for my past immersion in white male culture. I have looked for a diverse representation but still end up with a bunch of old white men! At least I've covered some important women and a couple of Asians and historically significant Blacks.

I apologize for these shortcomings.

As a lad, Byron Kennard came under the influence of a charismatic Sunday school teacher who made a pet of him and who instilled in him the desire to always do the right thing. The impressionable boy vowed, when he grew up, not only would he do the right thing himself, but he would work to instill the desire in others.

As a young adult, Byron became a community organizer, a job he conceived of as *instilling in others* a desire to always do the right thing. His focus was environmental protection. In the 1960s, he travelled the country forming local citizen groups to fight environmental pollution and helped lay the groundwork for Earth Day in 1970. His declared aim was to halt the further destruction of nature.

In the decades that followed, Kennard sparked a raft of environmental initiatives – organizing rallies and demonstrations, forming committees and coalitions, and founding several non-profit organizations. An inveterate scribbler, Kennard drafted countless screeds, published numerous jeremiads, sounded at least a dozen stirring calls to arms, and issued way too many manifestos.

Despite his labors, however — now, a half century later — the destruction of nature has not been halted; *but is picking up speed!*

All in all, that's sixty years spent trying to get people to do the right thing — and largely failing. It turns out people are not much inclined to do the right thing. Instead, they are preoccupied with other things: getting fed, getting laid, getting rich, and getting even with their enemies. Alas, most people don't have much time or energy left over to do the right thing. Bummer!

Kennard is also a history buff who's read thousands of books during his lifetime. In so doing, he had a singular purpose. As a passionate devotee of the common good, he was seeking to discover how social progress was achieved in the past, given the disinclination of most people to behave as they should.

Here, to his delight, Kennard discovered, down through time, audacious political leaders and bold social dissidents have frequently employed deviousness to lure people into doing the right thing, whether they want to or not. He's collected dozens of examples of what he calls "benevolent trickery," which make up this book.

Today, Kennard can usually be found at home with his nose stuck in a history book, trying to discover new ways to trick people into doing the right thing. He is now researching the experience of the Japanese under the Tokugawa shogunate (1603 to 1867).

Byron Kennard is the author of *You Can't Fool Mother Nature: The Once and Future Triumph of Environmentalism* (Amazon, 2020), a book written to commemorate the 50th Anniversary of Earth Day, of which he was a principal organizer.

ACKNOWLEDGMENTS

The design and production of this book was entirely in the super-competent hands of Joe Handy, who also designed and produced my previous book, *You Can't Fool Mother Nature,* published earlier this year. In both cases, the results are splendid; and, beholding the finished products, I am filled with pride and joy.

Joe, you make my words *look good*! What would I do without you?

Every word in this book has been sweated over not just by me, but also by Glenn Pinder, my lover, spouse, and creative collaborator. His hand is evident in all my varied endeavors, including the countless follies that I perpetuated over the decades.

Glenn, you've made me happy throughout our life together — now at 56 years and counting. What would I do without you?

Much of the thinking that's gone into this book was prompted by the many long conversations about history and politics that Glenn and I have enjoyed over the years with Gordon Binder and Michael Rawson, our best friends and fellow history buffs.

I thank you guys for continually subjecting all my flights of imagination to your well-intentioned, but trenchant, scrutiny and skepticism. What would I do without you?

NOTES ON THE IMAGES

Augustus Caesar - Statue "Augustus of Prima Porta" created in the 1st century is today part of the Vatican Museum

Charles de Gaulle - Strolling down the Champs-Elysées following the liberation of Paris, 1944

Ellen DeGeneres - Emmy winner. Photo by Alan Light, 1997

Frederick Douglass - Retouched photo taken in his 20s

Elizabeth I - Probably painted from life, circa 1575, this is known as the Darnley portrait on display at the National Portrait Gallery in London

Benjamin Franklin - From a carbonic alloy engraving, drawn by C. N. Cochin in 1977, engraved by A. H. Richie

Mahatma Gandhi - Gandhi spinning in the late 1940s

Mary G. Harris (Mother Jones) - Photo by Bertha Howell, 1902

Joan of Arc - An illustration from a manuscript by artist Jean Pichore, 1506, on display at the Musée Dobrée in Nantes

Except for where otherwise noted, these image files have been identified with the help of Wikipedia as being in the public domain.

How to Trick People into Doing the Right Thing

Lyndon B. Johnson - Signing the 1964 Civil Rights Act as Martin Luther King, Jr. and others look on

Byron Kennard - Photo by his friend Vivian Spiegelman

Abraham Lincoln - Scholars believe this portrait taken eleven days before the Gettysburg Address is the best photo ever taken of Lincoln, by Alexander Gardner, 1863

Louisiana Purchase - Map by William Morris, Portland State University, 2015

Douglas MacArthur - Photographed at his first meeting with Emperor Hirohito by U.S. Army Lt. Gaetano Faillace, 1945

Richard M. Nixon - Photo of meeting with Mao Ze-Dong from the National Archives and Records Administration, 1972

Mrs. Ronald Reagan - The First Lady and the President. Photo by Dennis Brack, 1988 (rights purchased from Alamy Stock Photo)

Richard III - 16th century portrait now part of the National Portrait Gallery in London

Franklin Delano Roosevelt - Classic public photo, 1944

Socrates - The Death of Socrates, currently on exhibit at the Metropolitan Museum of Art. Oil on canvas, Jacques Louis David, 1787

Charles Maurice de Talleyrand - Caricature "The Turncoat," drawing, 1815 (rights purchased from Alamy Stock Photo)

Greta Thunberg - Speaking at the European Parliament, 2020

Harriet Tubman - An albumen photograph by Tabby Studios in Auburn, NY, circa 1880-1900

Mae West - Publicity still for the film "Go West Young Man," 1936

IF YOU LIKED THIS BOOK, YOU'LL *LOVE* ...

> ### *You Can't Fool Mother Nature: The Once and Future Triumph of Environmentalism*

"Byron Kennard's new book is a riveting, rollicking history of the environmental revolution, filled with insights that are rare, fascinating, and amusing."

— **Geoff Webb**, Former Political Director, Friends of the Earth

"This book documents how Earth Day actually emerged and honors all those involved over the years, a tale well told by Byron Kennard, the mastermind and master networker who pulled us all together and was a force of nature in steering the environmental movement!"

— **Hazel Henderson**, Founder, Ethical Markets Media, LLC (Cofounder in 1964 of Citizens for Clean Air in New York City)

What a tour de force! Really a wonderful memoir of the environmental movement as well as an homage to Earth Day 1970."

— **Dan Esty**, Professor, Yale Law School and Yale School of Forestry and Environmental Studies

Now available in paperback & ebook

Amazon.com/author/byronkennard

"Byron Kennard is unique among social change activists in that his expertise is based on the real world of social change combined with his incredible knowledge of history. "

— **Rich Tafel**, Founder of The Public Squared; Author, *Party Crasher: A Gay Republican Challenges Politics as Usual*, and the founder of Log Cabin Republicans

"This is an elegant and funny book that only a devoted history buff like Byron Kennard could have written. No one but Byron could link Earth Day so perceptively to the Renaissance, the Reformation, and French Revolution, and to great leaders like Edmund Burke and Winston Churchill. In doing so, he offers up a long view, which we Americans don't have as a rule, and a way to put the daunting challenges of the present into a useful historical perspective."

— **Cathy Lerza**, former editor, *Environmental Action* magazine

"Bold, upbeat, and witty — but behind the drollery, Kennard is shrewdly advocating the pursuit of radical ecological goals through conservative methods, signifying a sea change in thinking about the politics of the environment."

— **Peter H. Schuck**, Professor Emeritus, Yale Law School; Author, *One Nation Undecided: Clear Thinking About Five Hard Issues That Divide Us*

"Back in the 1960s, I was one of the grassroots organizers working alongside Byron Kennard and other green pioneers to create a new consciousness about the urgent need to protect the environment. We succeeded, and in spades too! Ultimately, the seeds we planted grew into one of the great social and political movements in history, winning the adherence of millions of people the world over."

— **Brock Evans,** President, The Endangered Species Coalition

You Can't Fool Mother Nature: The Once and Future Triumph of Environmentalism

"Kennard's book ... reads as a measure of love, for the environment as for those who have served it."

— **William K. Reilly**, Former Administrator, U.S. Environmental Protection Agency (1989 - 1993)

"Byron writes in a style that leaps off the page with wit and humor."

— **Francesca Lyman**, investigative journalist, author, *The Greenhouse Trap*

"Earlier today I picked up You Can't Fool Mother Nature. There went the schedule! I simply couldn't put it down!"

— **Bill Drayton**, founder and chair of Ashoka: Innovators for the Public; Assistant Administrator of EPA in the Carter Administration

Now available in paperback & ebook
Amazon.com/author/byronkennard

Treat Yourself !

www.ingramcontent.com/pod-product-compliance
Lightning Source LLC
Chambersburg PA
CBHW070805240726

48654CB00007B/220